Information handling in museums

Elizabeth Orna and Charles Pettitt

Information handling in museums

 K G Saur • Clive Bingley
New York • London • München • Paris

First published 1980
by Clive Bingley Ltd, a member of
the K G Saur International Publishing Group
Copyright Elizabeth Orna

Designed by Graham Stevens
Text set in 10 on 11pt Theme Medium
8 on 9 Univers Light and Bold

Printed and bound in the UK by
Redwood Burn Ltd of Trowbridge and Esher
Bingley (UK) ISBN 0 85157 300 2
Saur (USA) ISBN 0 89664 440 5

Orna, Elizabeth
Information handling in museums
1) Museum techniques
2) Information storage and retrieval systems
I) Title   II) Pettitt, Charles
069   AM111

ISBN 0 85157 300 2

Contents

Acknowledgments

It is a pleasure to acknowledge the help of many people in museums and other institutions who provided detailed information and useful advice, in particular:

Brighton Museums
Dr A Smout
Keeper of Geology, Booth Museum

British Museum
D McCutcheon
Principal Research Fellow
Department of Ethnography

British Museum (Natural History)
Dr M Hills

Castle Museum, Norwich
Dr M Rajnai, Keeper of Art
Dr Sue Margeson, Archaeology Dept
Mrs Rosemary O Donoghue

City of Birmingham, City Museums
and Art Gallery
Dr B Abell Seddon, Keeper
Natural History Department

Hancock Museum
University of Newcastle on Tyne
A M Tynan, Curator
Sue Turner, Geology Dept
M Daly
I Webster
P G Robson

Hunterian Museum, Glasgow
Dr I W MacKie
Assistant Keeper in Archaeology

Imperial War Museum
R Smither
Dept of Information Retrieval

Museum of English Rural Life
University of Reading
R D Brigden, Keeper

National Maritime Museum
Dr J Cutbill
Information Retrieval Officer

Norfolk Archaeological Unit
E J Rose

North of England Open Air
Museum, Beamish
F Atkinson, OBE, Director
Rosemary Allan
Keeper of Social History
Ruth Dodds
Photographic Archivist
Trish Hall

Rye Museum
G S Bagley, Hon Curator

St Albans Museum
Sheila M Stone
Keeper of Documentation

Science Museum
Dr L D Will
Science Museum Library

Sedgwick Museum
Dept of Geology
Cambridge University
M Dorling
Dr D Price

Tudor House Museum,
Southampton
A B Rance
Senior Keeper of Museums

University of Manchester Museum
C Pettitt
Dept of Zoology

Dept of Museum Studies
Leicester University
G D Lewis, Director

Museums Association
Miss B Capstick, Secretary

Standing Commission on
Museums and Galleries
A D Heskett, Secretary

Aslib
J Martyn

I am particularly indebted to Richard Light and Andrew Roberts
of the Museum Documentation Advisory Unit, whose invitation to
give a seminar on indexing for museums provided the opportunity
to develop the ideas from which this book grew.

Thanks are also due to Graham Stevens for designing the book, and
for observations on the typographic design of museum documentation,
and to Bernard Orna for example material and critical comment on
the text.

Foreword
by Frank Atkinson
Director Beamish North of England Open Air Museum

Despite the oft-repeated aphorism that 'those who can't communicate should shut up!', it seems evident that a growing number of words are being spoken and books written on this complex matter of communication.

And the more we learn about the theories of communication the more does it become clear that we have a long way to go before we can communicate efficiently.

Meanwhile the jargon grows . . . word processing, data transfer systems, data processing, multi-terminal modules . . .

As for the documentation of our museum collections, imagination has, until recently, been able to feed on such an unappetizing pabulum as IRGMA or perhaps the more palatable GOS. Now we can whet our appetites on a thesaurus, hopefully more satisfying than that curiosity concocted by Roget.

But to be serious, I was delighted — and honoured — to be invited by Liz Orna to introduce her thoughtful and thought-provoking book. She has investigated the many experiments which, one is excited to see, are taking place up and down the country in all kinds of museums — and has discussed their merits and demerits.

Until recently one could have been forgiven for believing that the time was drawing near when we should begin to walk along some common documentary pathway, but the rapid strides now being taken in the field of information processing may open up still further uncharted lands. Perhaps we should not finalize all our techniques until we know just how much more these exciting new studies have in store for us. After all, if we had arranged our cataloguing systems to satisfy the clumsy demands of the early 'mainframe' computer, we should now be at an unnecessary disadvantage when faced with the relative freedom of the video display and the floppy disc.

But Liz Orna's book will help us see much more clearly what it is that we have been striving to achieve. More and more, we need someone like her to stand back and point out the obvious and I, for one, thank her for her logical approach and welcome this addition to the library of the cataloguer and communicator.

1

Chapter 1
Introduction

Before I could read, I had become hooked on museums. The Sunderland Museum and the Hancock in Newcastle are among the earliest pleasures I can recall, and the pleasure in museums has lasted ever since. When I became professionally concerned with the problems of handling information contained in printed documents, I was intrigued to find that ways of information handling much used in that field were little used when the information was contained in objects housed in museums rather than in books housed in libraries. I was also interested to observe that methods of handling information in museums ranged from those characteristic of the early nineteenth century to those drawing on the technology of the late twentieth — and indeed that examples of the opposite ends of the range could be found next door to one another, sometimes within the same museum.

These observations were confirmed by people from within the museum world. A proposal (Roberts, 1975) for a survey of cataloguing practice in British museums, based on a preliminary sample study, spoke of ' . . . an alarming lack of awareness of basic information storage and retrieval techniques among museum curators' and of 'often grossly insufficient' resources devoted to analysing and recording museum objects; many museums were found to fall short of the minimum recommendations of the Wright Committee (DES, 1973), that is, an adequate catalogue and classified card indexes.

Nor is the problem confined to British museums. It is a theme that runs through an international issue of *Museum* devoted to the applications of computers. Homulos (1978), writing from Canada, makes a statement typical of many others from different countries: 'In the average museum, documentation *per se* often receives a very low priority, presumably because of its low visibility. Documentation is the product of many people: registrars, curators, conservators, etc; it thus varies according to the professional interests, as well as the personal approaches, of the individuals involved. The result is that the documentation of a collection is often very uneven and rarely integrated into a complete system.'

This book grew from the belief that information is information, whatever the physical form in which it is embodied — book, artefact, building, or site — and that those concerned with handling it in any one form should be able to draw profitably on ways of thinking about information problems that have proved useful in any other. The emphasis on *ways of thinking* is important; it is not a matter of borrowing equipment or techniques, but of being aware of what one wants to do with information, capable of analysing one's own information-handling problems, and able to make sound choices of techniques and equipment with which to implement a system based on the analysis. This is in accord with a dynamic rather than a static concept of what information is. Information is that which is capable of transforming the structure of ideas by means of communication between human beings for useful purposes. It thus implies a transaction between those who have knowledge about something and those who need the knowledge in order to do something with it. In the transaction, those on the giving side structure the knowledge so that those who receive it can use it to change the structure of their own knowledge.

Indexing selected itself as a key topic in the development of this theme, because the questions one needs to ask and answer in deciding how and what to index are central to the whole question of finding flexible ways of handling information for active use. For our purposes, it is convenient to take a broad definition of indexing, as any means of gaining freedom of access to records that represent things, and of acquiring flexibility in manipulating those records in order to get the information we want out of them. It is a topic that has been less discussed than that of recording, in the upsurge of interest over the past decade or so in museum information retrieval.

The practical and theoretical work of the Information Retrieval Group of the Museums Association (IRGMA) and more recently of the Museum Documentation Advisory Unit (MDAU) in developing documentation standards for structuring data on museum objects, and in popularizing record cards for various disciplines which embody those standards, has raised the consciousness of museum staff about the necessity for standardized and meticulous recording, and has stimulated further development even among those museums which have decided against using the IRGMA/MDA documents.

The present activity in computerizing museum records, pursued in various ways in many different centres, has great potential for helping museums to achieve active and economic use of their collections. Like most powerful tools, however, computer use has also great potential for compounding existing difficulties and creating new ones of far greater magnitude; computers can make chaos a great deal faster than can unaided human beings.

3

If staff in museums which adopt computerization do not have the chance to do their own preliminary thinking about what they want to get out of the system, how they want to handle information, and what future developments they want the system to be capable of handling, then the museums will not benefit much, and neither will their staff or the users of the museums. Unfortunately it can happen that the people most affected are not even aware until too late of the need to do this kind of preliminary thinking and to make sure it is taken into account by those who design the systems. In the worst case, they never become aware of the need, and become incomprehending and hurt or hostile victims of a change they have not had the chance to understand.

If, on the other hand, there is rigorous thinking at the start by museum staff about the information-handling questions involved in indexing, the intellectual effort of solving them will pay off in various ways. Museum workers who have done this will be better equipped to deal with information retrieval and hence to exploit their collections more actively, even if computerization is not the ultimate solution in their case. If a computer system *is* introduced, they will be in a better position to achieve mutual understanding and professional respect with computer specialists, and so improve the chances of the successful introduction of a computer system that is an improvement on the system it replaces. This kind of consciousness raising about information handling can also lead in the long term towards a bringing together of the curating and documentation aspects of work, both within museums and between museums and related libraries. Some pioneering steps have been taken in that direction; if they can become the rule rather than the exception, the division mentioned at the beginning of this chapter will be overcome, to the profit of both kinds of institution.

At the present time, progress towards full exploitation of information resources can have survival value too. Storehouses of knowledge which is inaccessible to those who could make it productive are sad places at any time. As the then Director of the Leicester University Department of Museum Studies said ten years ago 'It is a poor sort of museum which has unique information locked up in its collections and records, unobtainable because it has no organized method of retrieving it.' (Singleton, 1969). When public expenditure on the arts and on education is under pressure, making knowledge accessible has an additional importance. If museums are to survive and justify their right to public funds, they need to be able to show that they are able to exploit their resources of information fully and economically. The institution that can show that it is well used and increasingly used, and that it is cost-effective, is in a good position to gain continued financial support.

● References

Department of Education and Science *Provincial museums and galleries* Report of a committee appointed by the Paymaster General HMSO, 1973 (the Wright report)

Homulos, P S 'The Canadian National Inventory Programme' *Museum XXX* (3/4) 1978, 153–69

Roberts, D A 'Proposals for a survey of cataloguing practice in British museums' *Museums journal* 75(2) September 1975, 78–80

Singleton, R 'What should we train our curators to do?' *Museums journal* 69(3) 1969, 133–4

Chapter 2
Tools for information handling: how catalogues, classifications
and indexes developed; how they complement one another

' "Yes," said Mr Brooke, with an easy smile, "but I have documents.
I began a long while ago to collect documents. They want arranging,
but when a question has struck me, I have written to somebody and
got an answer. I have documents at my back. But now, how do you
arrange your documents?"
"In pigeon-holes partly," said Mr Casaubon, with a rather startled
air of effort.
"Ah, pigeon-holes will not do. I have tried pigeon-holes, but
everything gets mixed in pigeon-holes; I never know whether a
paper is in A or Z."
"I wish you would let me sort your papers for you, uncle," said
Dorothea, "I would letter them all, and then make a list of subjects
under each letter." '
George Eliot, *Middlemarch*, 1871, ch2

● The central problem of information handling

Mr Brooke was presenting the central problem of information
handling, and Dorothea was suggesting a solution to it (one which
was not accepted; Mr Brooke thought young ladies too flighty to
deal with documents, but he would have done well to accept his
niece's offer). It is a problem confronted by many people in the
course of their work — from individuals with a collection of stamps
or porcelain, to store keepers responsible for keeping stocks of
spares, office managers in charge of filing systems, librarians, and
museum curators.
    Those whose business it is to house and care for physical
objects — whether they be Greek statuary, ancient musical
instruments, military relics, or documents of any kind — always
come up against the inconvenient fact that an object can physically
be in only one place at a time. This is inconvenient because, in order
to be able to think about an object purposefully in relation to other
objects — which is the business of the users of museums, libraries
and all the other kinds of collections mentioned — it is necessary to
be able to bring together and manipulate the information content of
the objects. This means finding some way of representing objects

which allows them to be moved around freely, by proxy, as it were, so that they can be brought together in any way that suits the kind of thinking we want to do about them, whether it is to compare particular characteristics, or to count how many there are of a specific kind, or to identify items having a given group of features in common.

● Freedom of access

The problem is essentially one of getting the maximum freedom of access to the useful information contained in the objects, at the minimum cost in terms of time, effort and money. The purpose of that freedom was well expressed in respect of books a century and a quarter ago by Crestadoro (1856), a learned and thoughtful frequenter of the British Museum library.

'How can an alphabetical Catalogue on the existing plan of joint inventory and index, or one entry and one heading, satisfy inquirers that seek the same book from different data, and for different purposes?. . . Freedom is, in all things, an essential condition of growth and power. The purposes of readers in search of a book are as manifold as the names and subjects, or headings under which the book may be traced. Entering the book only once is giving but one of its many references and suppressing the remainder; — it is serving the purpose of one reader and defeating that of others. So far the book is withdrawn from the public, its light is extinguished and destroyed.'

● Two major aspects

The purpose of this chapter is to look at the two major aspects of this problem: the record that represents the object, and the ways of gaining access to and manipulating the records for useful purposes. The development of ways of dealing with them — particularly in libraries, where the subject has been most intensively studied — will be outlined, and the functions of catalogues, classifications and indexes defined, as a basis for discussing, in the next chapter, the questions that must be answered before decisions can be taken on how to handle information. Figure 2.1 shows in diagram form the problems considered in this chapter.

Figure 2.1 Problems of objects and records

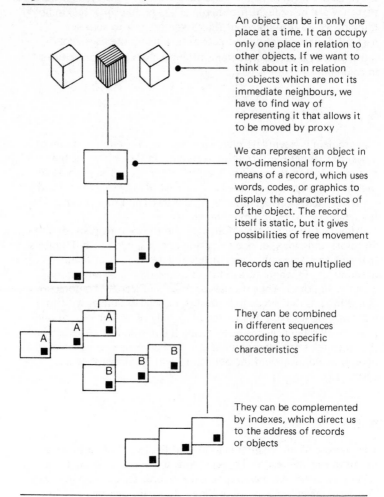

An object can be in only one place at a time. It can occupy only one place in relation to other objects. If we want to think about it in relation to objects which are not its immediate neighbours, we have to find way of representing it that allows it to be moved by proxy

We can represent an object in two-dimensional form by means of a record, which uses words, codes, or graphics to display the characteristics of of the object. The record itself is static, but it gives possibilities of free movement

Records can be multiplied

They can be combined in different sequences according to specific characteristics

They can be complemented by indexes, which direct us to the address of records or objects

● Stages in dealing with the problem

There are various stages in dealing with the problem. Historically they have tended to follow the sequence described below, though at the present time early stages can be found co-existing with more developed ones, either because they meet the purpose adequately or because the utility of more developed methods has not yet been appreciated.

● *The object on its own*

In the first stage, the objects themselves are the only repository of information. They are arranged in some way, which may be random, or in order of acquisition (for example, books put on to a shelf as they are bought), or based on some principle of organization (for example tinned goods kept on a different shelf in the kitchen cupboard from cake-making materials). In this stage, finding and using the objects depends on the user's knowledge of the stock. Very remarkable results can be obtained, but they depend on feats of memory and are dependent on anyone who wants to use the objects remembering how they are arranged.

● *The object represented by a record*

The next stage is the representation of the object by a record of it which describes its characteristics in some way and which thus acts as a surrogate for the object. The record may be very brief and selective, or it may be a full and meticulous description of the provenance, appearance, material, date, state of preservation etc of the object. The way in which whatever information the record contains is organized can vary too: it may be quite informal, and vary from time to time according to the preference of the person who prepares it, or it may be highly structured, with quite complex rules governing its preparation.

Figure 2.2 shows examples of instructions for the preparation of records relating to books (A) and to museum objects (B). The first is from the standard rules used in libraries for cataloguing printed materials. Even though the information to which the rules are applied is all contained within the document which is being recorded, the rules are highly complex. The task of record preparation is a great deal more complicated with museum objects. It can involve identification and evaluation, as well as the application of rules like those shown in the second example. The record may also need more data elements than are normally called for in the cataloguing of books, eg material and process of manufacture, ownership history, condition, and citation data.

The importance of the record cannot be over-estimated; it represents the object and so carries a central responsibility in any system of handling information. What has not been put into the record cannot be retrieved. Inconsistencies in the presentation of information in the record, for example calling similar objects at one time by one name and at another by a different name, or spelling the same author's name differently on different records, will lead to failures to find like objects, or to delays and confusions. This is true whatever the system of information handling, whether it is a simple manual one, or one which uses on-line computerized retrieval

Figure 2.2A Example of rules for library cataloguing from Anglo American Cataloguing Rules, second edition Library Association, 1978

21.34A Enter court rules governing a single court (regardless of their official nature, e.g., laws, administrative regulations) under the heading for the jurisdiction enacting the law and add a uniform title (see 25.15A) to the added entry. Make an added entry under the heading for the agency or agent promulgating the court rules.

> Rules of practice and procedure of United States Tax Court. Main entry under the heading for the court
>
> Lord Chancellor's Office. The rules of the Supreme Court, 1965
>> (The rules of the English Supreme Court, promulgated by the Lord Chancellor's Office; an administrative regulation)
>
> Main entry under the heading for the court
> Added entry under the heading for the office
> Added entry under the heading for the United Kingdom
>> with uniform title for the regulation

Figure 2.2B Example from IRGMA/MDA rules for completing record cards from Decorative arts card instructions Museum Documentation Association 1979 (reproduced by permission of the MDA)

Keyword and Detail Separators

Five types of separators are needed within a box when recording keywords and detail. They may be used in any sensible combination.

The first is to separate keywords. You should use either an ampersand '&' or an asterix [sic] '*' for this KEYWORD SEPARATOR.
> eg   black & blue
> Roberts & Light
> Cardiff & Edinburgh
> 1970 & 1976

In each of these cases both terms are considered as keywords suitable as INDEX HEADINGS.

The second separator is to distinguish a keyword from its detail. You should use the round brackets '('and')' as DETAIL SEPARATORS. The detail may precede or follow the keyword to which it refers but cannot be in the middle! For example:
> (pre) 1875
> 1875 (pre)
> black (tinted at edge) & (in part) blue
> Capstick (Museums Association)
> Canterbury (near)
> (near) Canterbury

(computer use has indeed done good service to manual systems by highlighting the importance of scrupulous quality control of records).

The implications of the importance of the record are twofold:
1) careful thinking in the planning stage about what information should go into a record
2) established and carefully observed rules and procedures for preparing records (in the museum field, a great contribution has been made here by the Information Retrieval Group of the Museums Association — IRGMA, and its successor the Museum Documentation Association — MDA).

● *The records combined into a list*
Long before these modern developments in the records themselves, various ways of combining records evolved. The first step was usually a simple list, relating the record to a description of the place where the object it represented was kept.

Such lists constituted elementary catalogues. Like the objects themselves, they might be arranged in various ways: for example, in order of acquisition, in order of location, or by some other principle such as by subject, or alphabetically by name of object or author, or by material. The arrangement of the list might correspond to that of the objects, for example both list and objects in order of acquisition, with the most recently acquired item in last place; or it might be different, for example the list in order of acquisition and the objects arranged by subject or author — in which case the list would have to give some key to the actual location of the objects.

A single listing of the objects in a collection has the advantage of being more quickly scanned, with less physical movement, than a collection of objects, but it has disadvantages. As each record appears only once, there is only one easy way in to the information contained in the list, and that is through the way in which it has been arranged.

There is also the physical difficulty, with lists arranged in any order other than that of acquisition, of inserting new items in their proper place; this leads to interlining and repeated transcribings to keep the list up to date. The straightforward list, with each record appearing only once, is therefore an imperfect way of bringing together records which represent objects.

● *Separation and multiplication of records*
The next step has usually been a more sophisticated list, with each record on a separate piece of paper or card. That allows the record representing the object to be moved about at will, and to be copied. The ability to move records makes it possible to re-arrange them to accommodate new ones in the correct place in the chosen

11

arrangement, or to reflect new decisions about arrangement. The possibility of multiplying them allows records to be put in a variety of arrangements simultaneously. Hence it is possible to have one set of records arranged according to the features they have in common, so that the records of all books dealing with the theory of management, or all objects associated with the blacksmith's craft, are brought together; another set arranged alphabetically according to the names of the donors of objects, or the authors or titles of books; and yet another arranged to place — details of all the buildings in given parishes, or of all coins issued by particular mints.

The separation and multiplication of records marks a great advance; it confers increased power and freedom by virtue of the multiple ways into the store of information which it provides.

● Classification

It seems possible that this physical development in the form of records may have contributed to stimulating the development of theories about classification of documents which was such a feature of librarianship from the late nineteenth century onwards.

Human beings have of course always classified objects and concepts; organizing one's ideas according to common features is one of the fundamental activities of the human intelligence, which permits generalization and abstraction, and so extends the power of the mind. Besides the everyday rough and ready classifications we learn in childhood and extend later for day to day purposes, there are the broad general classifications which philosophers have from classical times created to demonstrate their personal view of the universe, and the elaborate hierarchical classifications — of minerals, plants, fossils and animals, for example — which were constructed as scientific observation and investigation developed.

The classification of documents in libraries is a special case of the same kind of activity. Defined by Mills (1967) as 'the systematic arrangement of works according to their thought content', it has led to many developments which are still relevant to information handling, whether the information is contained in printed documents, or in objects, even in a period when the possibilities for computer applications in information handling are developing so rapidly.

It is necessary to draw on librarianship for an exposition of the purposes, advantages and problems of classifications because little has been done in the way of developing classifications or the related theory in museums. (As late as 1960, the Museums Association *Handbook for museum curators* (Museums Association, 1960), in its section on registration and cataloguing, made no reference to classification.) While museums with collections in the field of natural history have made use of the existing classifications in such disciplines as botany or geology, very few classifications have been specially designed for museum use. Two — from the Museum of English Rural Life at Reading University, and from the North of England Open Air Museum at Beamish, are briefly described in Chapter 9.

● *How classification helps the user*
The basis of library classifications is the choice of features by which items in a collection of documents are grouped together and placed in sequence. Having clear principles for grouping and ordering is an enormous advantage to those responsible for the collection. It helps them to make consistent decisions about where to insert new material; it aids them in deciding where to start seeking items that fulfil particular criteria; and it acts as a 'prompt' to remind them of related areas which may also yield relevant items. Ordinary users of a library, faced with finding their own way around the collection, also benefit from this guidance, as embodied in the arrangement of books on the shelves, or in the records representing them which are arranged in a classified catalogue. The utility of library classifications is increased by the use of a coding — a 'notation' — which represents the classes of the system in abbreviated form. The notation has its inbuilt rules, which ensure that items classified by the system are put in the correct groups and filed in the correct sequence; for example, in an alphabetical notation, items coded 'A' would go before those coded 'B'. The use of the notation as part of each record representing an item brings together the records of related items so that they can be considered together, and guides the user to the physical location of the items.

Grouping items into classes according to the features they possess demands decisions on relationships:
what are the significant features which relate one item to others?
(in considering animals, for instance, is the native element of the animal the significant feature, in which case bats are grouped with birds, and whales with fish; or is it the physical structure, which puts both with the mammals).

● *Traditional classification*
The great traditional classifications, of which Dewey's Decimal Classification is the best-known example, start from a 'universe' of 'entities' (things or ideas) for the subject matter under consideration — in the case of Dewey, 'all areas of specialized knowledge and activity developed in modern society' (Mills, 1967). The first grouping of the entities — the terms 'universe' and 'entities' are those of Ranganathan — is achieved by dividing them according to the

Figure 2.3 Example of a 'family tree' classification

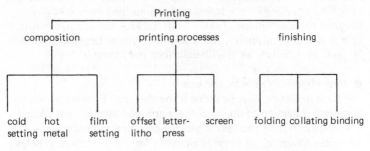

The first grouping is according to the stage in the total printing process; it is in chronological sequence of main activities.

The second grouping, within each main activity, is according to the technique used.

features considered of most significance for the matter in hand. The next grouping is applied by dividing the groups so produced according to the next most significant feature. These sub-groups can again be sub-divided in the same way. The results of this kind of operation give a structure similar to that of the traditional family tree, as shown in Figure 2.3.

● *Disadvantages of traditional classification*
Like the traditional family tree, traditional classification expresses only two kinds of relationship: the 'father-son' relation between the elements at one level and those 'descended' from them at the next; and the 'sibling' relationship between the groups subordinated to any one parent group. Any grouping is immediately subordinate only to the one above it. Each item that is classified in such a system has only one class assigned to it. There is no possibility of reflecting a combination of subjects in an item by a combination of different classes.

This kind of hierarchy has in fact some of the disadvantages of the feudal system which it resembles. It is somewhat static, and hence has difficulty in accommodating change, in the shape of new concepts not in existence when the classification was devised, or of new groupings resulting from advances in knowledge. While there is no problem in assigning a class to items which deal with one subject which exactly coincides with, or can be assimilated to, a grouping in the classification, there is a problem, not unlike that experienced by

Procrustes' guests, when works deal with a combination of subjects which occur in different groupings in the classification, ie when they embody relationships other than those of subordination or strictly bounded co-ordination.

● *Difficulties overcome by faceted classification*
These difficulties have to a large extent been overcome by a more flexible, logical and subtle approach to the design of classification, embodied in the idea of 'faceted classification'. The theoretical basis for this approach was laid by Ranganathan (1937, 1945). A brief and practical exposition is given by Vickery (1960, p12), who describes the basis of faceted classification as 'the sorting of terms in a given field of knowledge into homogeneous, mutually exclusive facets, each derived from the parent universe by a single characteristic of division.' For example, in the general class engineering industry, there could be facets for:

Facets	Examples of terms
materials	steel, copper, titanium
forms of materials	sheet, bar
processes applied to materials	cutting, grinding, welding
machines/equipment used for carrying out the processes	lathes, milling machines, drills
products resulting from the application of processes by machines to materials	turbines, washing machines, castings
occupational groups of people engaged in using machines or other activities that lead to the manufacture of products	technologists, technicians, craftsmen, operators

The process is in part similar to what goes on in the construction of a traditional classification, and within the facets the ordering is traditionally hierarchical (for example under the term 'lathes' in the machines/equipment facet quoted above, there could be a subordinate group of terms for different types of lathe: capstan lathes, centre lathes, copy lathes, turret lathes etc.)

It differs from traditional classification in three ways, as Vickery points out. In the first place, the analysis of the subject area carried out in order to construct the classification is very rigorous. Secondly, the facets that make up the classification are 'not locked into rigid, enumerative schedules, but are left to combine with each other in the fullest freedom, so that every type of relation between terms and between subjects may be expressed.' (Vickery, 1960, p13). Finally, faceted classification allows the expression of relationships other than those of hierarchy and subordination which are the only ones provided for in the traditional classification, and so permits classification which reflects the content of works dealing with compound subjects. The freedom so gained is accompanied by safeguards to ensure consistency in classifying, in the form of very precise rules on the order of combination of facets and on the use of the notation which stands for the terms of the classification.

● *The in-built problem of classification*

While faceted classification solves many of the problems associated with traditional classification, there remains one inbuilt problem, arising from the very nature of classification: any principle of arrangement will separate some like things in the very process of bringing others together (a problem quaintly known in library circles as that of the 'distributed relative'). A simple example makes the difficulty clear.

If a social history collection in a museum classifies tools by the materials of the crafts in which they are used, tools of the same basic form which are used in different trades are separated from one another: a flint knapper's hammer from a silversmith's, a thatching needle from an upholstery needle. So anyone who wants to compare the form of all hammers in the total collection has a long task. He will have to think of all the possible hammer-using crafts and go to the appropriate section of the classified catalogue and scan card by card, looking for hammers.

● The index as the solution to the inbuilt problem of classification

The problem is not an insoluble one. All that is needed to overcome it is a system which complements the classification's arrangement and which makes it possible, in one way or another, to bring together and inspect records which have one or more common features but which are separated by the principle of arrangement used in the classification. Dewey found such a system in the 'relative index' to his classification, an alphabetical subject index which he claimed to be, 'the most important feature of the system' (Dewey, 1885).

It is indeed impossible to over-estimate the importance of indexes as devices which allow freedom of movement into records that represents things, and flexibility in manipulating them in order to get the information we need.

Two main kinds of indexes should be distinguished: indexes to classifications — like Dewey's relative index — which tell us at which 'address' we should look to find works on given subjects or combinations of subjects; and direct indexes to the contents of the store of information. Figures 2.4—2.6 give examples. In either case they are *complementary:* they do not repeat the content of the records which stand for items; instead, they give the address either of the records, or of the actual items. Crestadoro (1856, p10) makes the distinction very well between records and the index to them: 'The first must enter as full and as strict an account of every article, individually, as will identify it at once and prevent mistaking it for any that might happen to be like it. The second needs only to refer to its inventorial number. By the one you are actually placed in the presence of the very object you seek, as far as its full description is concerned; by the other you are given its address.'

Indexes are also complementary in arrangement, as well as in form. The principle of arrangement is the one best known to the whole population, the alphabetic. The apparent simplicity of access through alphabetic arrangement makes it tempting to question whether it is necessary to go to the trouble of classifying. Why not just index? The temptation is particularly strong when one has access to electronic means of processing data which can so readily sort the data input into any given sequence.

In fact, if one approaches the problem of information handling from the indexing rather than the classifying end, the necessity for some kind of classification soon presents itself. In order to help the indexer to make consistent indexing decisions and the user to find related things, it is necessary to find some way of grouping the concepts being indexed; a purely alpha arrangement will not do by itself. As Crestadoro observed in working out the logic of his proposed scheme on the 'Art of making catalogues in libraries' (1856, p 25), it was necessary to give every heading in the index its own hierarchical class list in order to show users the topics related to the one they sought. The ultimate result of this process, he perceived, would be a 'complete classification of all the contents of the library'.

Figure 2.4 Index to schedules of UDC Special edition for education. FID 374, The Hague, 1965

```
Trade(s) unions 331.88
Tradesmen, training 377.3
Trading (business, technique) 658.6
Tradition(s), ethnography and folklore 39
    sociology 301.173
Traffic (control, organization) 656 Cf. Transport
    routes, planning 711.7
Training (education) 37 Cf. Education; Schools; Teaching
    forms of 371.3
    professional, vocational 377
    teachers 371.13, 377.8
Training (military) 355
    manoeuvres, exercises, etc 355.5
    officers 355.23
Training (sports) 79.091, 796.091
Transitions to secondary school 373.4
    from secondary school to university 373.58
```

Figure 2.5 From a 'chain index' to a library's use of UDC classification. Mills (1967, p170)

Dyestuffs for terylene (667.2[1])

Chain		Index entries	
6	Technology	Technology	600
66	Chemical	Chemical technology	660
667.2	Dyeing	Dyeing: technology	667.2
667.2[1]	Textiles	Textiles: Dyeing	
	Artificial fibres	Technology	667.2[1]
		Artificial fibres: Dyeing:	
		Technology	667.2[1]
		Terylene: Dyeing:	
		Technology	667.2[1]

The left-hand list shows the subject analysis of the content of a book classified and added to library stock, with the UDC class numbers alongside. The right-hand list shows the entries made on the basis of the analysis in the library's index of its use of UDC class numbers. The index is used by library staff to maintain consistency in their classifying; it also acts as a guide to catalogue users in locating books on specific subjects.

Figure 2.6 FEU information system manual Further Education Curriculum Review and Development Unit, 1978. Post-coordinate index to a small information system. The item numbers on the 10-column cards lead the user direct to items which contain information on the subject with which the cards are headed. The cards can be used to search for information either on single subjects or on specific combinations of subjects (see p).

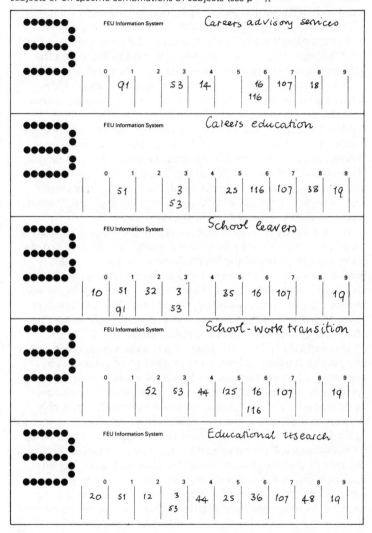

A contemporary review of indexing theories as formulated by information scientists concerned with computerized information retrieval (Borko, 1977) reaches a not dissimilar conclusion, expressed in rather more opaque terms:

'According to Salton, a quality index is one that will result in high recall and high precision and will produce, for any given collection of documents, a clustering of similar or related items . . . These definitions of index quality are instructive, for from them one can infer that indexing can be made more effective by increasing the cohesion within clusters and the separation between clusters.'

In the museum field, an interesting article by MacKie (1978) relates a development in the thinking of museum cataloguers who started from compiling a list of generic names ('Simple Names' in the MDA system) in the fields of archaeology and ethnography, and finished by finding that they needed to develop a classification.

'There was . . . a severe disadvantage in the whole idea of a Simple Name list, in that the only useful way a general catalogue of these could be produced was in alphabetical order. In that case closely related items like "boat" and "sledge", or "clothing" and "footwear" would be widely separated in the catalogue.

It was eventually realised that the problem was being approached from the wrong end and that what was needed was an even broader framework than that of the Simple Names — some even more general classification of artifacts into which everything should logically fit somewhere and without strain. The only really possible general classification, it was clear, would have to be one based on function and the solution devised was to introduce the concept of Major Categories above that of Simple Names.'

It is particularly interesting that this process was found necessary in a project designed to lead to the production of catalogues by computer. The use of computers for handling the records that represent objects can indeed help to remove some of the rigours associated with the construction of classifications. It is probably unlikely that any more universal classifications of this kind produced in the late nineteenth and early twentieth centuries will be developed. Classifications will probably go on being needed in special fields, and the type of analysis associated with the construction of faceted classifications will remain valuable; the computer can help with the subsequent sorting and verifying operations, and can obviate the need for devising expressive notation by which to order records and items. In the present situation, the analytical techniques of classification remain essential, but the way into information handling through indexing is becoming the easier one. It is at the same time the one which has had least attention paid to it, and for both reasons there will be a strong emphasis on it in ensuing chapters.

● Summary

An *object* can be in only one place at a time.

In order to think about it in relation to other objects it is necessary to *represent* it in such a way that the representation can be freely moved about.

The representation is a *record* which gives essential details of the object.

Records are one of the essential parts of any system of *handling information.* They are the inputs to the system, and what is not included in them cannot be retrieved and output.

There must be established and carefully observed *rules* for creating records.

In manual systems, records can be most easily manipulated if each record is *physically separate* from other records.

Lists of records in which each record appears only once are not a good vehicle for information handling; a complete pass through the list has to be made to find items meeting any criteria other than those according to which the list was compiled, and it is difficult to accommodate new items in lists.

Multiplication of records on individual cards or pieces of paper allows several arrangements in different sequences, and hence greater freedom of access to the information they carry and more power for the user.

Both lists and single or multiple arrangements of separate records can be called *catalogues.* A catalogue is a collection of records representing objects, arranged in some way.

One principle of arrangement of individual records, and of the items they represent, specially developed in libraries, is the *classification* Classification involves grouping together related concepts according to some common feature into *classes* and *hierarchies.*

Items added to a classified collection are assigned to a place in the classification according to rules established as part of the classification. Their place in the classification is noted on their records by means of *notation.*

21

The records are arranged according to the notation to form a *classified catalogue,* and the items themselves are physically placed in sequence according to the notation rules of the classification. Problems of the rigidity of traditional hierarchic classifications are largely overcome by *faceted* classification, which permits greater freedom in assigning items of compound content to a place in the classification.

The built-in problem of classified arrangement — that *it separates some like items by bringing together others* — can be overcome by *indexes.*

Indexes *complement* classifications, and classifications complement indexes.

Indexes are a means of gaining *maximum freedom of access* to the contents of a collection of records, or to a collection of items, or to a classification.

The index refers the user to the *address* of a record or an item or a class in a classification. It *does not repeat the content* which is given at that address.

● References

Borko, Harold 'Toward a theory of indexing' *Information processing and management* 13(6) 1977, 355—65

[Crestadoro, A] *The art of making catalogues of libraries or, a method to obtain in a short time a most perfect, complete, and satisfactory printed catalogue of the British Museum Library* by A reader therein The Literary, Scientific & Artistic Reference Office, 1856

Dewey, Melvil *Abridged decimal classification and relativ index for libraries, clippings, notes etc* Second edition, Boston, 1885

MacKie, E W 'A hierarchy of artifact names for the MDA cards' *MDA information* 2 (6) September 1978, 55—9

Mills, J *A modern outline of library classification* Chapman & Hall, 1967

Museums Association *Handbook for museum curators. Part A Section 1 Administration,* 1960

Ranganathan, S R *Prolegomena to library classification* (first edition) Madra Library Association, 1937

Ranganathan, S R *Elements of library classification* N.K. Publishing House, Poona, 1945

Vickery, B C *Faceted classification. A guide to the construction and use of special schemes* Aslib, 1960

Vickery, B C *Information systems* Butterworths, 1973

Chapter 3
Defining information needs

It will be evident from the last chapter that each of the gains in freedom of access to information is bought at a price: the more freedom and power one seeks, the greater and more costly the effort that needs to be put into planning to achieve it, into analysis, and into recording. The aim must always be to get the outputs that are really needed at the lowest cost and in the simplest way that meets an acceptable proportion of the need. For example, if we are able, with an existing system, to meet 60 per cent of our information needs, and if, by adding 5 per cent to the time spent on information processing we can improve that to meeting 80 per cent of our needs, it will be well worth putting in the 5 per cent extra effort. But if we then look at improving performance still further, and find that to push up the 80 per cent success rate to 90 per cent would demand a 25 per cent increase in the time spent on information handling, the return is less attractive, and unless there are very strong reasons for seeking a higher success rate, and few restrictions on resources, we are likely to decide against investing so much more time.

Before we can make any rational decisions about information handling, therefore, there are a number of questions to be answered. Without finding the most reliable answers we can manage, there can be no certainty that time and resources put into developments in information handling will yield corresponding benefits.

The approach recommended in this chapter is a systems one, that is, it looks at all aspects of the handling of information as they relate to one another, rather than in isolation. The value of doing this lies in the fact that it helps towards seeing the potential for integrated, rather than piecemeal, exploitation of resources. Bergengren (1978) points to the need for this approach in museums: 'Very few museums have information systems that as a whole work satisfactorily. Most museums have some subsystems that are very useful and others that are not. Besides, certain subsystems, which ought to be found in the museum, are missing. However, the biggest problem is not whether the individual subsystems function, but the fact that there is noco-ordination of their activities.' The systems approach is often thought of as being exclusively a computer technique; it is in fact a straight-forward and commonsense way of looking at problems, which pays off whether the end result is computer use or not.

● What are the purposes of the museum's service?

First, it is necessary to define the purposes of the service the museum seeks to offer, because they will form the criterion for assessing present systems of information handling and for planning developments. This is not to say that it is impossible for museums with different objectives to use similar tools for information handling, and it is obviously an economic advantage if they can get certain bits of their system 'off the peg' (MDA cards, or computer programs, for example) rather than having to start from scratch with every bit of it. What it does mean is that there is no substitute for careful initial thinking by those responsible for museum policies. This is the best guarantee of achieving an information-handling system that does the job it is required to do, and of being able to make good use of facilities available from outside.

So the questions to be thought about first are on these lines:
Does this museum aim to
— maintain complete and authoritative collections in its own fields?
— provide representative collections in a number of fields?
— cover a single specialized field in depth?

Who are the people it is designed to serve:
— researchers and scholars?
— the general public?
— teachers and students?

What level of initiative does the museum seek to take in its relations with them:
— making collections available for research?
— responding to specific inquiries from the public?
— running educational activities for the public and for young people at school?
— publishing scholarly works based on the collections?
— general interest publishing?

Within each section of a checklist of this kind, there may well be a number of affirmative answers — many museums, for instance, take all the initiatives listed above. In that case, it is also necessary to decide which are the most vital to the museum's purposes — which would be the last to be sacrificed if the museum were put to the necessity of sacrifice and still sought to maintain its identity.

● What does the existing system consist of?

The next question is: what does the existing system consist of? This makes the starting point from which we can identify what needs improvement, what is not provided for at all, where duplication or overlap exists, where information may be leaking away un-noticed through gaps, and where existing information can be more fully exploited with little extra effort. It is useful to give this investigation some structure, which will yield a coherent picture of the flow of information. A chronological sequence of the activities running from acquisition onwards is a useful framework. It can take the form of a simple chart, like the one in Figure 3.1.

This should give a picture of what is being done at present, by whom, with what resources, and for what purposes. It is essential to get the explanations of procedures etc from the people who actually carry them out, because they know how they work and are often able to question features which serve little useful purpose, or to suggest changes which would improve the system. It is also essential to collect examples of the forms, cards, and other documents used in the system. The scale of operation also needs to be known: the present size of the collections being studied, the annual rate of addition to them, and the average rate of processing items — how much time from staff of the various grades concerned does it take to process an item through all the stages from acquisition to file creation? how long does the average search take? what proportion of curatorial time is spent on searching and the activities that follow from it?

● How data are used

The next step is to examine the use to which data available from the collections are put. Use is one of the most important criteria against which existing systems and procedures, and possible new ones, must be evaluated. If they do not meet an existing or likely future use, their utility is very doubtful, no matter how intrinsically pleasing they may look.

Typical answers to the question of use might be that data from the collection are used:
— for research, by researchers on the museum's staff and from outside, involving such activities as studying the evolution of products, or the development of a particular industrial process, comparing specimens of given organisms, or making statistical analyses of large numbers of objects of similar origins

26

Figure 3.1 Chart of information-handling activities

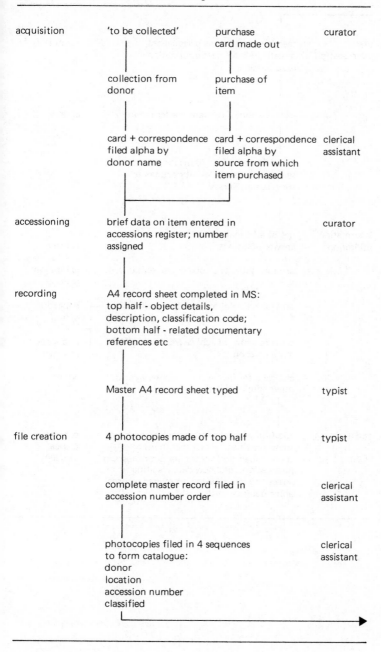

acquisition	'to be collected'	purchase card made out	curator
	collection from donor	purchase of item	
	card + correspondence filed alpha by donor name	card + correspondence filed alpha by source from which item purchased	clerical assistant
accessioning	brief data on item entered in accessions register; number assigned		curator
recording	A4 record sheet completed in MS: top half - object details, description, classification code; bottom half - related documentary references etc		
	Master A4 record sheet typed		typist
file creation	4 photocopies made of top half		typist
	complete master record filed in accession number order		clerical assistant
	photocopies filed in 4 sequences to form catalogue: donor location accession number classified		clerical assistant

Figure 3.1 continued

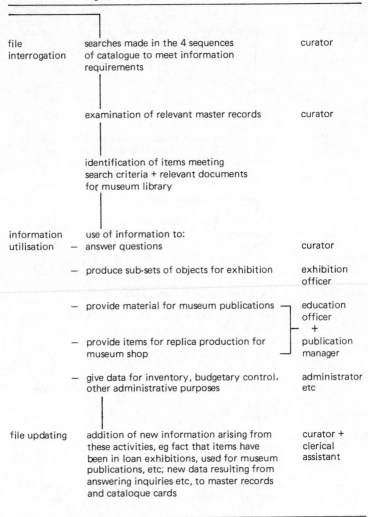

file interrogation	searches made in the 4 sequences of catalogue to meet information requirements	curator
	examination of relevant master records	curator
	identification of items meeting search criteria + relevant documents for museum library	
information utilisation	use of information to: — answer questions	curator
	— produce sub-sets of objects for exhibition	exhibition officer
	— provide material for museum publications	education officer + publication manager
	— provide items for replica production for museum shop	
	— give data for inventory, budgetary control, other administrative purposes	administrator etc
file updating	addition of new information arising from these activities, eg fact that items have been in loan exhibitions, used for museum publications, etc; new data resulting from answering inquiries etc, to master records and catalogue cards	curator + clerical assistant

— to answer inquiries from the public
— to meet requests for information from other museums
— for putting together collections for special purposes, like a
programme of exhibitions, contributions to other people's
exhibitions, or travelling collections for schools
— for helping teachers to prepare project material
— for scholarly publication of monographs etc
— for popular and educational publications — booklets, brochures,
postcards, worksheets, quizzes, etc
— for programmes of lectures and demonstrations
— to prepare expenditure and other statistics as part of financial
control and budget preparation
— to control inventory for insurance and security purposes.

● Identifying the difficult areas

Having analysed how information is handled at present, and how it
is used, the next thing to look at is whether there is information
which it would be useful to have, but which at present either cannot
be got at in any way, or could be obtained only at an uneconomic
cost in staff time. In planning future development, it is essential to
know the failures in the present way of doing things. If in fact the
analysis shows no real information failures, and an acceptable ratio
of staff time and effort to necessary information outputs, one can
stop there, in the knowledge that the system is adequate for present
purposes. In that case, the only other questions to consider concern
the future development of the museum and its services. The factors
involved can be positive and negative — the latter could include the
effects of expenditure cuts, the former, plans to offer new services.

● *Problems with records*
Information failures and difficulties can arise at various points in the
process of information handling. If the accessions register is the only
record of data about items, the amount of data available is likely to
be insufficient to form a record which can stand for the item in
information handling. It can happen that the level of data input
varies from department to department within the same museum, so
that some departments limit their recording to brief details in the
register, while others prepare record cards in depth. The degree of
standardization of records can also vary with time. There may be
some from periods when minimal details were entered, others
prepared by different hands which are fuller but still informal, and
yet others which are highly structured. The variation in quality
affects their reliability as a surrogate for the objects they represent.

The amount of information input, even to highly structured records, may be inadequate for the purposes to which the museum puts its collections; information which has not been input in the first place can never be retrieved from the records and attempting to retrieve it in these circumstances places too heavy a burden on the knowledge and memory of curators.

The ways of producing records for related types of material may be different; for instance museum objects may be classified according to one classification scheme with its own notation, while the records relating to trade literature or photographs, which may refer to objects in the collection, may be arranged according to a different classification with a different notation. Here too, a heavy reliance has to be placed on the knowledge of the curators, and searching the records for information involves multiple strategies rather than a single one.

● *Lack of 'ways in'*
Most of the problems of information retrieval arise from the lack of sufficient ways in to the information content of the collection. If we take the example shown in Figure 3.1, the system performs well on accessioning and record creation, with a well-structured record form which contains all the necessary data about objects. The master record is used to produce a good quality four-fold catalogue, giving access by donor, location, accession number, and classification.

It breaks down when, as frequently happens, museum staff need to find items which meet criteria other than those of the four sequences of the catalogue. For example, they may be asked about objects made of a particular material, or manufactured by a particular process, or originating from a given period or from a given area. If the classification does not group items according to these features, the questions will demand knowledge, experience, serendipity, and a lot of hard slog through the catalogue. Similarly, a catalogue of pictures in an art department may permit easy access via artist's name or medium, but may fail when there is a need to find pictures of a specific content — eg representations of a building or a street in different periods, or of a particular industry.

If, as often happens, there is only a single master record, and the records are arranged in just one sequence, then bringing together information on groups of items with particular characteristics to meet the needs of inquirers is a slow process. For example, with a textile collection recorded in this way, it could be necessary to comb the register to produce handlists of categories which experience shows to be in demand — like embroideries, or particular items of costume, or clothing designed by particular couturiers. Production of each list will involve laborious transcribing, and that will not be the end of the matter, because, having located a relevant handlist for a specific inquiry, it is still necessary to sift through it to find items that meet the terms of the inquiry. For subject inquiries in fields where no handlist has yet been compiled it will be very difficult to get access to whatever information on the subject is contained in the records.

● *Failures in information utilization*
The stage of information utilization can also produce failures. It may be that there are purposes the existing information resources could serve, but for which it is not being used. There might for instance be a potential market among the museum's public for a series of small publications which could readily be met by using the existing ways of access to information about the collections. More commonly, perhaps, the lack of means of access prevents potential utilization of which museum staff are only too well aware. They may wish, for instance, that they could contribute to an exhibition on a particular country being mounted by another department by providing a display of typical flora, but be prevented because there is no way of finding records by country in the natural history collections; or they may know that there is a market for a booklet on representing of dancing on Greek ceramics, but have no means of finding examples in their collection which are decorated with representations of dancers. At an even more practical level, it may be impossible to use the records of the collection to spot what specimens have disappeared after a break-in, because there is no case-by-case inventory.

At the final stage, described as file updating in Figure 3.1, the museum's system may not provide for a standard way of adding new information to master records and to any files derived from them, and thus it will be impossible to be sure if any given record embodies the latest information about the object it represents — a change in attribution, for instance, or the conservation treatment it has been given.

● Identifying the ways in to information which are needed

Since the main failures and difficulties in retrieving information about items in collections usually prove on analysis to come from insufficient ways in to the information, (as Roberts and Light, 1980, put it, 'The need for a wide range of entry points to a single record remains a basic problem of museum documentation') the next step in analysing one's own existing system is to determine the ways in that are needed to answer the typical demands for information.

It is interesting that when we start analysing from this point of view we tend to finish up with a list of categories very similar to those produced in the development of a faceted classification (see Chapter 2, p15). Figure 3.2 shows in tabulated form some of the ways in to the store of information that are likely to be needed.

This analysis in effect gives a list of the facets of the collection which are of importance to its users. It can help in building a new system, or in rectifying the shortcomings of an existing one. It may lead to a decision to re-design record forms, so that the input provides for the kind of output needed. It also forms the framework into which we can fit the names of the terms we decide to use in recording and searching — the *indexing vocabulary*. More will be said about this in chapter 5; here it is important to observe again that making decisions about what to call things is made much easier by having the kind of framework which a series of categories provides (see Chapter 2, pp 17–18).

● How specific should guidance be?

The next step in analysis is to look at a different dimension in information needs: the degree of specificity that is required in answering questions from the store of information. Not only do we need to know what ways in are going to be required; we also need to be able to predict as accurately as possible the degree of precision that will be needed in signposting them. Will it be enough to give general directions, or will users need highly specific guides that will take them to the exact spot that contains just the information they need and nothing else?

The decisions we take in this matter are important, because they will affect the economy of the efforts put into information handling, and the effectiveness of retrieval of information. The art lies in trying to match the degree of detail used in signposting the ways in to the degree required by the kind of questions that have to be answered. If the questions are highly detailed and specific, but the ways in to the collection are signposted only in very broad and general terms, every search for fine detail is going to dredge up so much that is irrelevant that users will be poorly served. If, on the other hand, we know that in a given area the questions are mainly generalized ones, it is a waste of effort to signpost to a level of detail that will seldom if ever be required.

Figure 3.2 Examples of ways in to information which may be needed*

1	Persons	donors, collectors, historical figures associated with objects, people portrayed in pictures, etc
2	Entities	plants, insects, stones, birds, etc
3	Products of industries, crafts	locomotives, coins, swords, pots, clocks, bracelets, etc
4	Concepts	Hermeticism, gravity, Buddhism, the periodic table, etc
5	Properties	colour, dimensions, degree of completeness, shape, etc
6	Materials — naturally occurring, semi-processed, etc	sulphur, granite, bronze, porcelain, cotton, coal, etc
7	Processes — involving materials and leading to new products or materials	distillation, combustion, electrolysis, etc
8	Operations — performed by people on materials or entities to give products	carving, turning, embroidering, weaving, cutting, etc
9	Manufacture/production — industries and trades which organize the application by people of operations etc on materials etc to give products	bookbinding, shipbuilding, cooperage, bell-founding, chain-making, etc
10	Places	places of occurrence of minerals, sites where archaeological objects were found, places depicted in photographs, towns where items were manufactured, grid references for the occurrence of flora, etc
11	Time	dates or epochs of manufacture, periods of geological time, dynasties
12	Bibliographical details, forms	titles etc of relevant books & articles, bibliographic forms, eg trade catalogue, report, thesis, monograph, etc

*Readers interested in the theory of classification will note that this list corresponds to the five fundamental categories of Ranganathan: items 1 — 5 correspond to Personality, 6 to Materials, 7 — 9 to Energy, and 10 and 11 to the common subdivisions of Place and Time (12 is a form division)

If, for instance, a museum is devoted primarily to a major industry on which the economic and social life in its area have been largely founded, then very detailed treatment will be needed for every object relating to that industry; broader ways of access will suffice for those other aspects of the region which are less fully represented in the collections.

In case of doubt about the degree of detail that is required, it is safer to err on the side of being over-specific. While highly specific answers can never be achieved from highly general indexing,it is always possible to knock together a group of terms that have proved more specific than is actually needed, without any loss of information.

It is possible to use the listing of the ways in to information that are required (see Figure 3.2) as a checklist for deciding on how specific it is necessary to be. For each element in the list, it should be possible to predict from knowledge and experience of one's own collection the degree of detail needed to meet the demands for information. Thus, for example, if one needs to be able to find information relating to particular periods of time, is the appropriate period a millenium, a century, a year, or a month? If place of manufacture is a required way in, is region or county a sufficient key for extracting information, or must it be at the level of town, or of a named factory? It may well be that in some situations two or three levels of detail are all necessary for meeting differing requirements. Some users may be looking for generalized information, and some for specific, from the same collection. In such cases, the most specific level must be provided for, but in order to achieve economy and efficiency it is necessary to find ways of ensuring that those who are looking for a wide range of information on a subject have their attention drawn to items which deal with individual parts of the subject. Ways of achieving this are discussed later (see pp 61–62).

● What is the typical form of question?

The next stage in the analysis of information needs is to look at the typical form of the questions which have to be answered by reference to the collection of information. In essence, the questions directed to any file of information fall into two groups. Consider, as an example, the telephone directory as an information source. We use it in two ways: first to find the number of someone whose name we know; second, to locate firms or institutions which provide particular goods or services. For the first, we use the ordinary alphabetical directory, which lists names and gives the telephone number against each. For the second, we use the classified directory, which groups the entries under terms that represent the goods or services they offer. The two ways of arrangement are appropriate to the purposes the two directories serve; the first makes it easy to locate a number belonging to a named person, the second to locate someone who possesses certain attributes, like being a joiner or a coal merchant.

In using information about museum collections, the same two approaches can be observed. One names a specific object — say a picture, an archaeological site, or a microscope — because the inquirer wants to be able to use information about some or all of its attributes: the subject or style of the picture, the nature of the pottery finds from the site, the optical system of the microscope. The other approach is a search for objects — as yet unknown to the seeker — which have a certain attribute or combination of attributes: Lowestoft porcelain coffee pots; kitchen implements that would have been found in a Weardale farmhouse in the 1880s.

The importance of analysing the use of a museum collection from this angle lies in the implications it has for deciding on the appropriate means of organizing information. This point is discussed in the next chapter; here it is sufficient to say that failure to take into account the character of the questions can lead to the choice of methods which make it difficult to retrieve the information which is needed. The two types of approach are sometimes referred to as *item* and *feature* questions (Jolley, 1968). Item questions name an item (object) and seek its features (attributes); feature questions name features (attributes) and seek items (objects) which have these features.

Researchers using museum collections are often concerned with item questions; they know the objects they are looking for, and are interested in studying their features. Discoveries about the features of these items may then lead to the search for other items having similar features, for purposes of comparison — to feature questions. The public users of museums probably tend more towards seeking the answers to feature questions. Typical inquiries are for examples of given types of objects, rather than for one specific object. The 'identification' type of inquiry is really a feature question; in effect when an object is presented for identification the question being asked is 'here is an item with given features; what other items in the collection, or in the curator's knowledge, have this combination of features? what are those items? what class do they belong to?'

● A look to the future

The analysis made so far should enable us to identify the information needs in the existing situation, and the extent to which they are being met. We have part of the criteria for evaluating which are the most important needs, and for deciding methods of meeting them; these are supplied by our knowledge of the purposes of the museum's service to users, and of how they need to use information from the collections. To complete the criteria, we need to look to the future.

The simpler aspect of this is covered by the question — what is the growth rate of the collection? In some cases the answer may be nil — the museum may exist to house a finite collection, complete in itself, in which case the only problem is that of matching the means of information handling to its present size and to the uses that are made of it. In others, there may be a small and predictable annual growth rate from donations and a planned level of purchasing; what has happened over the past few years can be taken as an adequate guide to how the size of the collection will increase in the next few. Others again may be in a period of rapid growth — this is typically so in recently established museums covering a field not previously catered for. They may need to plan for a transition from one method of information handling — adequate for their initial small collection and capable of being managed by a small nucleus of staff — to a more sophisticated one, exploiting the resources of information more fully and demanding more staff time. Finally, there is the case of museums which face a discontinuity — after a period of small annual growth, they may find themselves about to acquire a large addition to their collections — by bequest, or by a museum merger, for instance — and this may provide the occasion for a complete re-thinking of the whole of their information-handling methods.

The more complex questions about the future arise from trying to predict the direction in which overall policy will move in the next few years. As mentioned earlier (see page 29), this may be positive or negative. Negative development is unfortunately a possibility (or, indeed, a probability) that must be taken into account. Since most museums are wholly or partly publicly financed, their development will always be affected by restrictions on central or local government spending. This is certainly the case at the time of writing, and the only sensible thing to do about constraints of this kind is to try to use them positively, so that savings can be achieved by more efficient use of resources while real needs continue to be met not less effectively, and if possible more so. This is not, alas, a counsel which can always be carried out, but the aim is worth pursuing. So far as information handling is concerned, the application of this kind of response to negative constraints will lie in deciding on priorities among information needs, and planning development to meet them as simply and economically as possible; in avoiding cuts which will result in permanent loss of information or in less efficient information handling; and in seeking to make the most cost-effective use of the skills and knowledge of museum staff.

The future may, happily, also include some wholly positive plans which lie within the resources of the museum. It may be in a position to implement a project for introducing a new subject area. There may be plans to develop links with other institutions in the area for joint use of resources, for instance by building up a teaching function in conjunction with local schools and colleges. The museum may be able to take advantage of such goverment aid to areas of high unemployment as the Youth Opportunities Programme or the Special Temporary Employment Programme to take on extra people for a period to carry through a project which can be of permanent benefit to its information handling. There may be plans to overcome the restrictions which public spending cuts place on growth by setting up a fund-raising programme among firms, organizations and individuals in its area. Or it may be planning to extend its publishing programme or to institute a museum shop in order to develop its public relations and bring in revenue.

All such developments would create new needs in the handling and retrieval of information. For example, links with educational institutions could mean museum staff needed improved access to information about the collections to support a programme of talks and demonstrations in schools, or that teachers needed an information retrieval system which they could easily operate themselves so as to identify materials they wanted to borrow for their own teaching projects. A fund-raising campaign could demand publications or small travelling exhibitions, angled to the aspects of the museum's collection relating to particular industries or to organizations like trade unions or chambers of commerce — and this would again demand a number of specialized ways into the collections. Not the least important criterion for deciding which information needs should be met and how to meet them is the staff resources available for information handling. The nature of these will condition the decisions that can be taken to a very large extent. No matter how pressing an information need or how desirable the results of meeting it, if there are not people to set up the machinery for meeting it or to maintain and develop it as demand grows, the need cannot be met. The effective utilization of manpower resources is discussed in Chapter 8.

● Summary

The steps in the definition of information needs are:

Define the purposes of the service offered

Analyse the existing system to show the present
flow of information

Examine the present use of data — who uses them
and for what purposes?

Identify present difficulties in handling information —
are they related to recording, to ways in to information,
or to utilization of information?

Identify ways in to the information which are needed

Identify how specific it is necessary to be in providing
ways in to information

Analyse the typical form of questions — do they name
specific objects and seek to know their attributes?
or do they name attributes and seek objects which
possess them?

Predict the growth rate of the collection

Assess the impact of plans for the future on
information needs

● References

Bergengren, G 'Towards a total information system' *Museum* XXX
3/4, 1978, 213–17

Jolley, J L *Data study* World University Library, 1968

Roberts, D A and Light, R B 'Museum documentation'
Journal of documentation 36 (1) March 1980, 42–84

Chapter 4
Organization for information retrieval: choosing methods to
meet the defined information needs

Analysis of the kind discussed in the last chapter provides the basis
for decisions about:
— how we organize data so that we can retrieve information readily
  in the ways we want
— the rules and conventions we shall need to use for putting in and
  retrieving information
— the 'hardware' that will be appropriate for the job in hand.

This chapter is concerned with the first set of decisions — on how to
organize the data; Chapters 5 and 6 deal with the other two. The
sequence of decisions is important. First, we need to be clear about
the conceptual question of the type of organization of information
that meets identified needs and fits the objectives of the museum's
service. After that we can go on to the conventions and protocols
that will allow the chosen form of organization to work smoothly
and consistently. Last of all, and on the basis of these decisions, we
can start looking for hardware which can help in performing the
tasks we have defined. All too often, the process is reversed, with
unfortunate results, which are discussed in Chapter 6.

The aspects of the analysis which are important for deciding on the
organization of data are:
— how data are used at present
— unmet information needs and information problems
— the 'ways in' to the store of data which are needed
— the typical forms of question which are put
— future developments which are envisaged.

● Implications of how data are used

What we know about use and users will particularly affect decisions
about the nature of the outputs that should be aimed for, and about
the kind of search procedures that users will be called on to operate.

● *Research use*
Research users, whether museum staff or from outside, can be
expected to know clearly what they are looking for, and to have
deep subject knowledge. They will need untreated rather than
processed data. Such users are likely to want detailed records from
which they can go direct to the objects represented by the record,
and they will probably need access both by item and by feature
(see page 35). They are unlikely to be deterred by methods of access
that involve observing fairly complex procedures and conventions,
but they will be happiest with a form of arrangement that coincides
as far as possible with the standard conceptual organization of their
subject field. This is especially so in natural sciences, where a
classified catalogue, following the accepted subject classification and
using the accepted modern terminology for the subject, is the obvious
first line of approach.

● *Inquiries from the public*
Public questions tend to be of the kind which want to know about
objects which possess given attributes (this includes identification
questions). For this kind of use, it is necessary to record to a level of
detail which is adequate for the bulk of the inquiries, and to be able
to interrogate the files of information according to given single or
combined attributes. Dealing with public inquiries can take a large
amount of curatorial time, which is thus not available for other
essential work, so the involvement of curators in this work should
be minimized by re-exploiting information assembled in answer to
past queries, for example by a simple form of index to answers, and
by monitoring trends in questions, so that the results can be fed into
the publishing programme. A cheaply produced leaflet or brochure
is likely to be a more cost-effective way of dealing with a frequent
type of question than is individual answering of each question on
the subject by a curator.

● *Requests for information from other museums*
For most museums at present, and probably for some time in the
future, the searches in response to such requests are likely to be
made by staff of the museum which receives the request, and
therefore no special requirements regarding search methods apply —
curators will, in the light of their subject knowledge and their
knowledge of their own system, interpret the questions into the
appropriate terms and find the answers, just as librarians do with
inter-library queries. In the early years of discussion about
information retrieval in museums, some emphasis was placed on
museums being able to get into and interrogate each other's files,
and there was talk of a 'national index' (Lewis, 1965) which would

allow any curator to scan the stock of any museum. Now, more realistic assessments prevail and while there is still a proper concern for inter-museum consistency where possible, the main stress is now placed on each individual institution making sure that it is as efficiently organized as possible to cope with its own information-handling needs. Those which are will find no difficulty in helping their neighbours.

● *Assembling collections for special purposes*
The same considerations as above apply about recording and ways in. In addition, if items are being brought together for particular uses like loan or travelling exhibitions, the information-handling system must provide for a routine of recording these excursions in the master records, and probably also for an index of institutions which have received such collections (which can record any who have proved careless borrowers!).

● *Helping teachers to prepare project material*
This kind of use could imply giving teachers themselves access to records, catalogues and indexes in order to indentify objects they wish to show as part of learning projects. This could have the advantages both of saving curators' time and building up the links between museum and education staff. To make best use of the situation, however, extra effort will probably need to be put into making the searching procedures simple, as occasional users, unlike every-day ones, are liable to find complicated procedures hard to cope with.

● *Scholarly and other publications*
For this kind of use, it is important to be able to relate ways of access to information to the requirements of the museum's publishing programme. It is also necessary to establish interaction between those who handle research, educational, and public inquiries and those who are responsible for planning the publishing programme, so that the programme can take account of developments in the use of the collections.

● *Programmes of lectures and demonstrations*
The same considerations apply as for publishing — ways of access to meet the likely requirements (which will be mainly by attribute) and utilization of feedback about user demands and interests in planning programmes.

● *Statistics for financial control*

If information about the collection is to be used for these purposes, it will be necessary for a record to give details of purchase price, date of acquisition and current valuation (it will probably be necessary for reasons of security to keep these data separate from other master record data and to control access to them). The file will need to provide access in various ways — for example, to the valuation and price of named items, to the valuation and price of items having certain attributes (bought by given departments, or relating to given subjects), and to the purchase price of items bought within a particular time period (as a check on the rate of utilization of the budget, or for establishing estimates for the next financial year). Providing for these ways in will also permit other statistical exercises of more general application — like the rate of growth of various departments, or changes over time in the importance attached to certain categories of objects.

● *Inventory control for insurance and security purposes*

This is a very important aspect of information handling from the point of view of those responsible for museum collections. To meet the requirements, it is necessary to be able to bring together information about value and information about location of objects. The master record should therefore carry a location indication, and there must be means of access to the records by location, so that, in the event of certain cases being broken into, it is possible to identify what they contained, and what is missing or damaged, and to go from that identification to the valuation of the items concerned.

● Positive indications from information problems

It was pointed out in Chapter 2 that the negative aspects of any system of information handling — the failures and the difficult areas — can provide positive pointers to improved ways of organizing for information retrieval. The problems can arise in three aspects of information handling: records, access to records to allow manipulation of data, and utilization of information. The first two are of special concern in this chapter; problems of utilization are mainly related to access and if the access difficulties are solved the utilization ones are in a fair way to being solved too.

● Problems with records

These can arise from:
— inadequate *quantitative input* of information
— inadequate or insufficiently controlled *structure* of records
— lack of *linkage* between different sets of records

The first step is to assess — from the analysis of ways in that are required — the essential content that must be input on master records. In many fields, one's own analysis on the lines of Figure 3.2, checked against the relevant MDA card and instruction booklet, should provide a reliable listing.

Next, it is necessary to find a structure which makes it easy
a) for the person creating the master record to do so as quickly and unambiguously as possible, with the minimum number of pauses for decision, and
b) for the person using the record as a representation of the object to get from it quickly and accurately whatever information is needed.

To achieve this demands a good deal of thought and experiment to find the format which meets both requirements. On the side of record creation, where often a number of people will be making inputs, it is important to check the sources of variance in the way a sample of people fill in a record for the same object, and to seek to minimize the variance by discussion, guidance, and training (see Chapter 8). So far as use is concerned, alternative formats should be tested by a sample of users to see which allows the speediest and most error-free retrieval of information.

The nature, and indeed the existence, of problems in the design of forms for these two purposes is all too often ignored; producing the form is regarded as a fairly routine job. It should not be, and it would be a great step forward if museum staff sought the aid of typographers concerned with information design for this aspect of their work.

Unfortunately the MDA cards which are widely used in museum recording today are not exempt from criticism on typographic grounds. Using green for printing the data does not help the legibility of the words. Green might be acceptable for the display line in the bottom left hand corner, but with the main data with an x-height of only 1mm, black ink on white stock would have helped legibility. There is some evidence to show that where very small types reach the threshold of legibility, capitals are more easily discriminated than lower case.

As shown in Figure 4.1 the way the data are organized demands a great deal of eye movement across the card. This means a greater searching time on the part of the person filling in the form, and

Figure 4.1 Section of a MDA card for the subject Decorative Arts

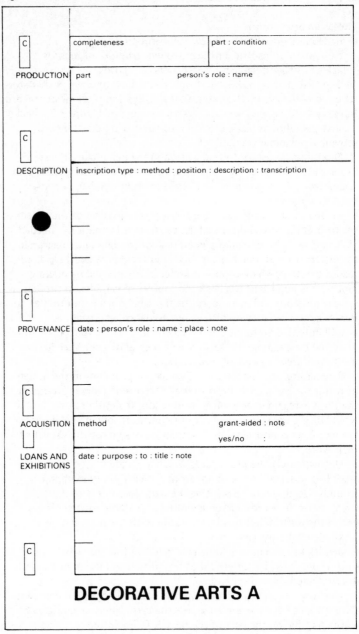

the same amount of effort is required by those who have to extract the data. The procedure of filling in and retrieving could have been made very much simpler if attention had been paid to this important aspect of the form design.

This leads directly on to the question of consistency in the placing of the data, the position and the amount of space allocated for those who have to fill in the card. It is not clear in many instances if the answers are to be placed underneath or alongside the questions. Forms should be organized typographically so that there is *sufficient* space to answer correctly and there should be no doubt about where the response should be. Readers who are interested will find a useful discussion of form design in Wright and Barnard (1975).

If the problem is one of linkage between sets of records, each of which performs adequately in its own field, it may be possible to indicate on the records in one set the coding of relevant records in the other. If two classifications are involved, this could be done by indicating reciprocal class marks. Otherwise it can be simply dealt with by having a place on records for the identifying numbers of relevant items which are covered by other sets of records. Figure 4.2 shows an example from an information system designed to give access both to the content of documents and to information about organizations and individuals. The master record for documents (not illustrated) allows the person completing it to underline the names of organizations and individuals associated with any given document. The underlining acts as an instruction to make entries for these in a separate index of organizations and individuals. As shown in Figure 4.2, the records in this index carry the identifying number of any documents held in the system which have originated from the organization or person concerned.

It is often the most efficient way of dealing with information to have separate files, organized in different ways, for certain types of information (for example, plain card indexes for names of persons or institutions can supplement punched feature card indexes — see Chapter 6, pp 79 & 82 — of subjects). For efficiency in access to such files, it is necessary to find a means which will allow any number of files to be searched by use of the same keys. This question is discussed in Chapter 5.

If changes in the content and/or structure of records are found necessary, the most practicable way of introducing them is to fix on a date from which they will be implemented (and to provide the opportunity for all the people concerned to be quite sure of the changes they will need to make). It may prove possible to have a planned programme of bringing in batches of the old records into the new recording system. Some museums have achieved this by the use of temporary staff sponsored by such government programmes as STEP (Special Temporary Employment Programme); others have found the opportunity, without increasing the staffing establishment, in a decision to computerize their information handling.

● Problems of access

The analysis will often show that the main problems with information handling lie in gaining access, in all the ways which users need, to the information contained in the records.

In some cases, the difficulties may be overcome by simply adding other sequences to the catalogue, that is, by multiplying the same master record to produce listings according to different keys, like the fourfold sequence shown in Figure 3.1. The listings can be either in the form of multiple card catalogues, or as printed-out lists. There are some interesting uses of word processors in this area being developed at present (see Chapter 6, pp 85–6 and Chapter 9, pp 154–5).

● How far classification can help

The approach through subject or attributes is the one that tends to cause most difficulty. In some subject areas, zoology, geology, botany, for example, an existing classification, as explained on page 13 , forms the preferred and most acceptable way in because it accords with the way in which the people using the collections think about the subject. In these areas, problems of access may be solved by a meticulously maintained classified catalogue, which will not need much in the way of complementary support from indexes.

In other subject areas, without an existing classification, it is, as explained in Chapter 2 (p20) usually necessary to develop, if not a full and rigorous classification, some means of ordering concepts, related to the ways in which the collection is used, which forms a basis for organizing the records. Such a basic framework can be devised from the analysis of ways into the information, like that shown in Figure 3.2. MacKie (1978) describes an example of this approach. The elaboration of a complete classification, at the Museum of English Rural Life, is described in Chapter 9 (pp 160–62).

Figure 4.2 Links between sets of records: entries from an index to individuals and organizations which direct the user to master records for documents associated with particular people and organizations

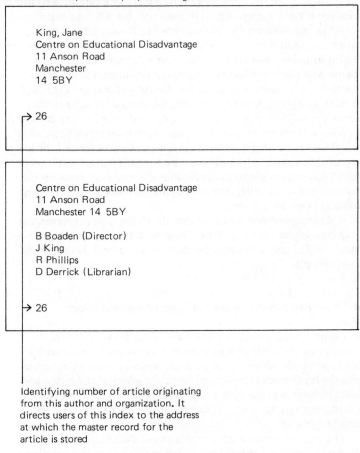

King, Jane
Centre on Educational Disadvantage
11 Anson Road
Manchester
14 5BY

→ 26

Centre on Educational Disadvantage
11 Anson Road
Manchester 14 5BY

B Boaden (Director)
J King
R Phillips
D Derrick (Librarian)

→ 26

Identifying number of article originating from this author and organization. It directs users of this index to the address at which the master record for the article is stored

● When indexes are necessary

This basic organization of concepts will normally need to be complemented with other devices which allow access through ways not provided by the framework — that is, through indexes.

The reasoning behind this requirement has already been outlined in different ways in Chapter 2 and 3 (pp 16 & 30—32). It may be useful to reinforce it here by a quotation from a pioneering article by Lewis (1965) who, at the beginning of the period of development of thinking about information handling in museums which led to the setting up of IRGMA and later of the MDA, expressed the essence of the problem from the point of view of a practising curator who had tried the classified approach on its own and found it wanting.

'While the museum owes its existence to the collections that it maintains, its usefulness and indeed its character derive as much from the information inherent in the specimens as from the specimens themselves. For the effective cataloguing of museum collections, therefore, it is essential to index the diversity of features exhibited by each specimen, be they chronological, geographical, historical, technological, topographical, typological and so on. . . The division of a museum index into mutually exclusive groups representing various subjects or museum departments should . . . be avoided and the ideal is probably a single information centre for each museum. Although such a proposal might be impracticable in a very large museum this does not prevent the departmental index from being based on this wider concept of indexing.'

It should be emphasized here that the simplest and cheapest way of generating indexes is to derive them from the master record so that a single input serves multiple purposes. Figure 4.3 exemplifies this principle.

● Organizing indexes to meet the type of question asked

In Chapter 3 the distinction was made (p 35) between two main types of question which are put to any collection of information: the type which names a given item and seeks to know its attributes, and the type which names an attribute, or group of attributes, and seeks items that possess these attributes. The two types are often called, respectively, item and feature questions. Figure 4.4 gives an example of each.

The type of question which our analysis shows to be the predominant one in the use of the collection will be a major deciding factor for the organization of indexes, as it is obviously economic to be able to answer with minimum effort the most frequent kind of question that is put. If most of the questions are of the feature kind, then the main organization of the index needs to provide for looking up features and finding the items that possess the features. If, for instance, we need to find all the blue lustre jugs made in Sunderland between 1840 and 1860 in our collection, we can quickly do so if we have entries (in whatever form, a point which will be discussed later) for lustre-ware, jugs, blue, Sunderland and 1840–49, 1850–59, followed by some way of identifying the items possessing each of

Figure 4.3 Use of a single input to provide catalogue sequences and indexes

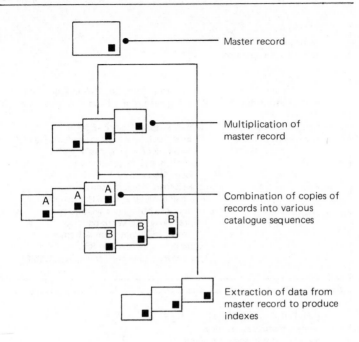

Master record

Multiplication of master record

Combination of copies of records into various catalogue sequences

Extraction of data from master record to produce indexes

Note: while records and indexes are here represented in card form this is only for convenience in drawing. The vehicle may indeed be cards, but it could be printed-out pages, computer print out, microform, computer output microform, or the data could even be held on-line on computer and called up on a visual display unit as required, without being printed out at all.

---

these features. All we have to do is to bring those feature entries together and extract the items which appear in all of them; by definition they will be blue lustre jugs made in Sunderland in those two decades.

On the other hand, if we had an index arranged by features alone, we should have difficulty in putting together all the features that made up a particular item we were looking for. If, for example, in a collection of photographs of buildings we wanted to bring out all those relating to a named building, and there were no index entries under the names of buildings, but only a set of features of buildings,

Figure 4.4 Item and feature questions

ITEM QUESTIONS
name an item
ask about its features

Example
item named   Lower Brook Street site, Winchester
item question asked   What has been found there during excavations?

features of the   Roman features from cAD50:
site named in reply   small temple, end of 1st century AD
                        water pipes, late 2nd century
                        workshop, late 3rd century
                        well, 4th century
          Post-Roman, Anglo-Saxon:
                        small cemetery, late 7th century
                        masonry building, c AD800 for
                        precious-metal working
                        timber buildings from Alfredian
                        replanning, cAD880—886
                        St Mary's Church, Tanner Street, 990AD

FEATURE QUESTIONS
name a feature or features
ask what items possess these features

Example
features named   Beads, faience, found in Egyptian tombs
feature question asked   What examples have we of these?

items with these   Specimens numbered JV1041 — JV1090
features named

like 'timber frame'. 'stone', 'dormers', 'hammer beams', with details
of the buildings possessing those features, we should have to scan
every record to see which referred to the building in question.

In practice, however, the choice is not a straight either/or. If we
are going to need to answer both kinds of question — and in most
information-handling systems both kinds are put — we can provide
both ways in, and for a little extra effort allow the searcher freedom
of movement in manipulating the records.

An example from an art department in a museum will show how
this can be done. The master record for each picture in the collection
is filed by artist's name; this constitutes in effect an 'item index'. It

is complemented by a series of feature indexes, for such things as persons represented in pictures, places, and other aspects of pictorial content. The entries in these indexes consist of the feature followed by brief details of the pictures embodying it, and the accession numbers. It is thus possible to find both pictures by named artists, and pictures which possess certain single features or combinations of features.

It should be noted that a feature index will usually give only a brief *address* of the items which possess a given feature — an identifying number, a classification code and perhaps an abbreviated description. An item index, on the other hand, will usually consist of the full records of the objects, arranged by some principle like accession number or personal name. In fact from the point of view of form an item index is identical to a catalogue sequence. The distinction quoted from Crestadoro (1856) in Chapter 2 (p 17) applies to feature indexes, not to item ones.

This combining of item and feature indexes, or of different sets of feature indexes, to allow both kinds of question to be answered by direct reference instead of one kind having to be answered by searching all the records in turn, makes a complete or conjugate index. If both kinds of answer are essential and needed often, the extra effort to make the index conjugate is well worth while, particularly if it can be done without a lot of copying information from one place to another.

One other division within feature indexes needs to be looked at — that is, between indexes which bring together the features possessed by items in a sequence determined by a set of rules (enumerative indexing), and those which leave the bringing together of features until the time when a search is required, when the features are picked out and put together to suit the question (post-coordinate indexing). Figure 4.5 shows an example of the two approaches.

The first approach is often used in the indexing of large collections of documents, as a means of specifying content very precisely. The highly structured indexing language used in the British National Bibliography — PRECIS — has strict rules for the sequence of terms designed to define the relationship between the features of each item that is indexed. The efficiency of indexes of this kind depends on the index terms being used in a prescribed form and no other. Indexers and searchers therefore have to learn a lot of rules to work with this type of index.

The other type is generally called 'post-coordinate'. because the features, instead of being tied together in a fixed sequence at the time of indexing, are co-ordinated at the time of searching. Fewer rules need to be learned here; the decisions needed are mainly about the vocabulary to be used to represent the concepts to be indexed, and the only guidance needed is for indexers and searchers on how to use the vocabulary. The question of vocabulary is discussed in Chapter 5; for the moment, the important point about this kind of index is that it can break down ideas into simple concepts which can be put together to form more complex ones.

The two approaches to indexing — enumerative and post-coordinate — have their own advantages and disadvantages. The first allows greater precision in indexing, at the cost of some rigidity and of the complexity of rules that have to be learned. The second is highly flexible and has simpler rules — at the cost of being less precise, particularly in its expression of relationships. Again, however, it is possible to some extent to have one's cake and eat it, to get some of the advantages of both methods, while avoiding the disadvantages by a little judicious borrowing. For example, some of the precision of the highly structured type of indexing can be acquired by post-coordinate indexes if we allow for using pre-coordinated terms for specific and often-used concepts.

A 'pure' post-coordinate approach would, for instance, break down the ideas relating to an object made of ivory inlaid with silver into three terms:

Ivory
Silver
Inlay

This could mean that a search for items of ivory inlaid with silver would also produce items of silver inlaid with ivory. A modification could be made to avoid this, if the collection had a lot of both kinds of item, so that irrelevant ones were not retrieved. Instead of three separate terms to index this type of item, one could use two pre-coordinated ones:

Ivory inlaid silver
Silver inlaid ivory

leaving Ivory and Silver for objects made exclusively of either material.

At the same time as indexing methods are considered, it is necessary to make decisions on the end product. The choice lies essentially between printed-out indexes in page form which can be used as a reference tool, and *ad hoc* searching of the actual index vehicles, ie the feature or item cards which constitute the index. In both cases the searches are likely to be two-stage — from the index to the record and from the record to the actual objects identified as meeting the search criteria.

The first is a good solution for those who can use the power of a computer to generate multiple outputs arranged according to different principles from a single record input, as the GOS package can, for instance (see Chapter 9, pp 160–62). The computer makes it

Figure 4.5 Two ways of indexing

Example of item being indexed:
ITEM L935 Sunderland lustreware jug

1 Fixed combination order of terms

Combination rule
1 general term for material
2 specific term for material
3 form of object
4 place of manufacture

Index entry
Ceramics
   Lustreware
      Jugs
         Sunderland L935

2 Post-co-ordinate index

No fixed combination order of terms. Index entry takes the
form of the item number written or punched on to cards which
are headed with the features. Features are co-ordinated at the
time when a search is made.

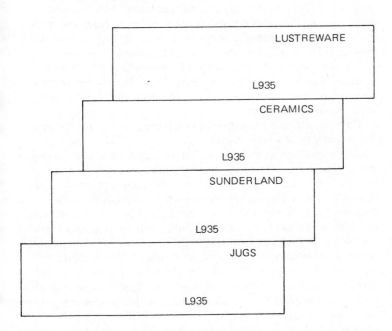

possible to update and amend the printed out index whenever required, as part of the process of editing the original records, and therefore it is an economic process. Similar, though more limited, possibilities of multiple printed-out indexes exist with the more sophisticated kinds of word processor (see Chapter 9, pp 154—6).

Lacking the capacity to produce multiple outputs quickly from a single input and to update them readily by a single operation, it is better to think of a feature type of post-coordinate index on cards (see Chapter 6). These can do the same job on *ad hoc* searches as a computer can, and are capable of producing results at least as quickly as a batched computer system

The nature of the physical forms which are appropriate for holding indexes — the 'vehicles' and the hardware — in manual systems is discussed in Chapter 6.

● Implications of future developments for data organization

Chapter 3 (pp 36—7) discussed the information implications of the predicted growth rate of collections, and of future policy changes — both externally and internally determined. Many of the decisions about meeting the needs created by foreseen future developments lie in the field of management, especially in the utilization of manpower resources. These questions are treated in Chapter 8. Here, it is sufficient to look at the implications for methods of information retrieval, bearing in mind that the feasibility of applying methods to meet future needs must depend on all the resources available, and in particular on manpower.

If the growth rate is going to be rapid over a period, for instance in a recently established museum, where there is likely to be initially a small nucleus of staff which will be added to as the museum proceeds with its development plan, it will be necessary to design an initial system which can be controlled with minimal resources. The system should be flexible enough to permit development as the information stock and resources to handle it grow, rather than being of a kind which will need to be dismantled and replaced by something completely different to meet the needs of growth. Recording should be set at a level where it can be maintained at a consistent quality without overstraining staff resources. This means planning a record form which can take all the detail that is envisaged as being ultimately necessary, and deciding on a manageable level for present entry. Then, over time, it should be possible to move towards more detailed recording, and, with luck, to go back over the earlier records in a phased programme and add the extra detail to them, to bring them to the same standard and the same information retrieval potential as the later ones.

Similarly, methods of handling the records for information retrieval should be planned for phased development. For example, one might decide initially simply to photocopy the master record to create donor, accession, and roughly classified sequences, with the aim of later developing a more detailed classification scheme and a complementary indexing system. During the period of growth, to aid reliable decision making on methods of handling development, it will be necessary to monitor the use of the collection, the types of questions that are put, and the degree of specificity they demand in answering.

If the main feature of future growth is a large quantitative and qualitative change caused by a major acquisition — which may have strings attached, making the deposit of the collection conditional on its being catalogued and made accessible within a given time limit, for instance — it may be advisable, as suggested in Chapter 3 (p 36) to use the change as the opportunity for thinking about possible new solutions to the total information-handling system of the museum. In such a case, the new collection could act as a pilot for introducing new methods, which could then be adopted in other parts of the museum. The appropriate approach would be to examine the nature of the new collection, identify the potential and the ways into it that are required, and to compare the resulting data with those from the analysis of information-handling systems at present used in the existing collections. It should then be possible to see how much of the present system could be used for the new collection, what new features are essential or desirable to meet the information-handling needs of the new collection, and how these features might be applied to improve information handling with the existing ones.

For more generalized future developments, the same principles of decision making about methods hold good: analysis of new needs/constraints that will be created; examining how they can be matched to existing systems; deciding on changes needed to meet the new situation, and how these changes can be made to benefit existing methods.

● Summary

The analysis of present information-handling systems can be used to aid decisions about how to organize data for information retrieval.

Different groups of users will have differing needs for output and differing capacities for using search methods. The final system should meet as many of the needs as possible from a single input of information.

Information problems and difficulties in using information can give positive indications for development.

Where the problem arises from records it is necessary to decide on the essential content and find a structure which aids both input and retrieval of information.

Where problems are related to access to data, it may be possible to resolve them by providing additional catalogue sequences.

Where the difficulties lie in the subject approach, a classification may help, especially in sciences which already have their own classification. Where no classifications exist, one answer is a basic framework for ordering ideas, complemented by indexes which allow multiple ways in and flexible exploitation of the full resources of the collection.

The cheapest way of generating indexes is to derive them from the master record so that a single input serves multiple purposes.

The way in which indexes are organized should depend on the types of question asked, whether they are predominantly *item* (naming items and asking for their features) or *feature* (naming features and asking for items which possess those features), or both. Usually both are needed, so *conjugate* indexes which allow searching in both ways are worth the effort. Often the main catalogue sequence can form the item index, complemented by feature indexes which repeat only minimal detail from the main entry.

Within feature indexes, two approaches to indexing are possible: *enumerative* indexing which brings features into a sequence according to fixed rules at the time of input, and *post-coordinate* indexing which brings them together in the required combinations at the time when a search for information is needed.

Implications of the future growth of collections should be taken into account in deciding on information retrieval methods.

● References

Lewis, G D 'Obtaining information from museum collections and
thoughts on a national museum index' *Museums journal* 65 (1)
1965—66, 12—22

MacKie, E W 'A hierarchy of artifact names for the MDA cards'
MDA information 2 (6) September 1978, 55—9

Wright, P & Barnard, P 'Just fill in this form — a review for designers'
Applied ergonomics December 1975, 213—20

Chapter 5
Vocabulary for indexing

'Descriptive terms tend to be applied inconsistently, with the same object being described in different terms by different recorders.'

'It became apparent that the committee felt strongly that some form of vocabulary control should be provided with the cards.'

'control of terminology was also felt to be important, and the committee agreed that lists of terms should preferably not contain the word "other".'

These poignant remarks, from accounts of discussions by some of the MDAU subject committees, reveal the awareness of museum workers — brought about by experience — of the problems that form the subject of this chapter. They had evidently realized that to have a structured record is only part of the answer to information retrieval needs, and that, in order to make sure we put in the things we are likely to want to get out, and get out what we want in the form we want it, a set of principles for decision making about terms is needed.

The problems are equally relevant for manual and computerized systems, though their importance for the former may, as Chenhall (1978) points out, have been fully revealed only by the encounter with the computer. Manual systems, he says, have broken down most often because 'they were not consistent in their structure and nomenclature, rather than that they were manual systems. Ever faster and more sophisticated techniques of processing verbal data have helped us to recognize, but not to solve the more basic problems of precision and consistency. We have now gone full circle and see that many of the catalogs previously maintained with manual systems of recording, storing, and retrieving information could have been substantially more useful than they were if the objects had been identified initially using a more precise system of nomenclature.'

The MDAU has not in fact responded to the appeal quoted above to provide vocabulary control with the cards. It has limited itself to drawing attention in its instructions to the importance of establishing conventions, and a recent article about the MDA system (Porter, 1978) makes it clear that this is a policy decision. 'Again, the establishment of controlled vocabularies must be left to users.'

This is a sound decision; a unit like the MDAU is in no position to produce recommended vocabulary for all the fields for which it provides record structures. What *is* lacking, however, is some help for museum staff on how to make their own decisions about vocabulary, in the light of their subject knowledge and their knowledge of the information needs they have to provide for, and on how to record the decisions and embody them in rules that will help in the efficient use of the vocabulary. This chapter seeks to give some straightforward guidance of this kind. Once again, readers are reminded that the way in which they interpret and apply it should be based on their own analysis of their information needs (see Chapter 3).

● Why vocabulary control is needed

In any situation where information has to be acquired, stored and used, it is necessary to make sure that:
1) a given thing is always referred to by the same name, so that nothing relevant is missed because a number of different names have been used in indexing the same thing
2) if people looking for information use different terms for the same topic, there is a way from each possible term to the topic in question
3) information can be found under the most precise term by which people are likely to ask for it, so that they do not have to plough through a lot of things they don't want before they get to the one thing they do want
4) people who are looking for a wide range of information on a topic have their attention drawn to items which are relevant to individual parts of it, or to related items which may have a useful bearing on it.
   It is particularly important that these conditions should be met when data are held in a number of separate files, so that all of them can be searched using the same terms; it is wasteful of time to have to use different access keys to different files. Manual systems in particular benefit from unified terminology, which reduces the effort inseparable from having to search files in sequence rather than simultaneously. Let us look at some ways of meeting the four requirements listed above.

● *Consistency in terms*
It is important to safeguard against the retrieval failures that occur if the same concept gets recorded at one time under one name and at others under different names.

The most frequent form in which this problem presents itself is that of alternative names for objects, processes, materials, etc. The alternatives may be between common and scientific nomenclature, between contemporary and earlier names, between names from different cultures, or between general and dialect names or names from different dialects. The choice of the standard term will depend on the nature of the collection, the way in which it is used, and by whom it is used, and on whether there are any existing standards for terminology for the subject matter in question.

● *Guidance to the standard term*
The method of ensuring that all the relevant items are retrieved, whatever the term by which they are asked for, is quite simple:

list the variants

decide on the standard term

record the decision, with
instructions to guide
users from the variants to
the standard term

Figure 5.1 gives an example. The standard term under which it is decided to index a given concept is often called an 'index term', while the non-preferred variants which are included with guidance to the standard term are referred to as 'entry terms', because they provide an entry to the information which is indexed under the index terms.

The same principle applies to the cases where differing versions of personal names, place names or names of institutions occur associated with items: the same provision as in the case of synonyms has to be made for a standard version and for guiding users to it from all the other versions.

● *Putting information under the most precise term*
It saves time and effort if those who search for information can find it under terms which are at the same level of detail as their needs. If we want examples of the late sixteenth century English embroidery known as blackwork, for instance, our task is simplified if 'blackwork' is an index term, and complicated if it is merely an entry term to the generalized index term 'embroidery' — especially if the collection of embroideries is a large one.

Figure 5.1 Guidance from entry terms to index term

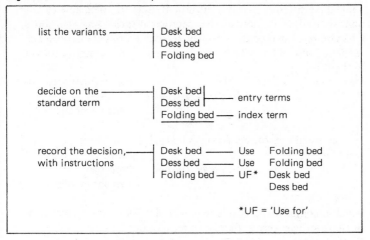

Decisions about the right level of precision are difficult to make, but they can be greatly helped by analysis of the type of question asked, as explained in Chapter 3 (pp 34—5). The other aid to decision is one's knowledge of the nature of the collections; as a general principle, those which are the most important and central to the purpose of the museum will need the most precise index terms. When in doubt, it is always safer to err on the side of precision rather than generalization.

● *Helping those who seek a broader view*
Not only do we need to provide access by the most precise terms under which users are likely to seek information. It is also necessary to help those who require a broader view of what the collection holds. For example, a user who seeks materials relating to the extracting and preparation processes used in the production of ferrous metals will need to be made aware of every such process covered by the collection, preferably without having to think up his own list of specific terms and then look up each separately. A simple but quite powerful device can help: if, when indexing items related to specific extracting/preparation processes — like open hearth, blast furnace, Bessemer converter, crucible, vacuum induction melting, cupola, etc — we index them not only under the particular process, but *also* under the general terms 'extracting/preparation processes' and 'ferrous metals', they will be retrieved, not only in specific searches for individual processes, but also in general searches for extracting/preparation processes as applied to ferrous metals.

61

To make sure that this device (sometimes call 'upward posting') is applied consistently — and it must be if users are to be able to rely on it — the decision needs to be recorded in such a way that those who compile the records from which index entries are derived are reminded of it. The writer's own preference is for an active reminder, in the form:

Open hearth	IAU *(Index Also Under)*	Extracting/preparation processes Ferrous metals

A more usual way of reminding indexers is in the form:

Open hearth	BT *(Broader Terms)*	Extracting/preparation processes Ferrous metals

which is complemented by a reminder alongside the 'broader term' of the 'narrower terms' that go to make it up; for example:

Extracting/ preparation processes	NT *(Narrower Terms)*	Bessemer converter Blast furnace Crucible Open hearth etc.

This form of instruction leaves it open for the indexer to decide whether to index under the more generic as well as the specific term. In making decisions on upward posting, the skill lies in judging how far up the hierarchy it is necessary to go in order to be helpful to users. The judgment must be based on knowledge of the material and of the ways in which it is used — without such knowledge, it is all too possible to take the process to ridiculous heights of generalization which will never be called for.

The other essential in helping those users who need a broader view is a means of directing their attention to related terms which may help them to find items relevant to a given search. To continue the example, those interested in processes of extracting and preparation are likely also to be interested in the products resulting. One way of directing their attention to other relevant information is to put a note into the master list of index terms:

Open hearth	SEE ALSO	Steel

or

Open hearth	RT *(Related Term)*	Steel

● The thesaurus — a structured vocabulary for indexing

In the discussion so far, reference has been made to building up a structured list of terms, which contains:
— index terms: the standard terms which it has been decided to use
— entry terms: the alternatives to the standard terms
— instructions and guidance: to help users of the list (ie the people who are responsible for indexing, and those who use the index when searching for information). The instructions have the function of:
1) pointing the way from entry terms to index terms
2) linking specific terms with broader ones
3) relating terms to other relevant terms

If indexing is to be successful and productive, it usually needs some such structured vocabulary, usually known as a *thesaurus,* which contains the terms used in a system of information, and the agreed rules for using them. The first thesauri produced for information retrieval were purely alphabetical listings, but experience showed that they gained in utility and power if they were founded on a conceptual structure, which brought together groups of related ideas, and if the alphabetical listing of terms was complemented by some kind of display of the structure. The reader is reminded of the discussion in Chapter 2 (pp 16—20) of the basic principles of classification and of how classification and indexing are mutually complementary and essential to one another, as tools for the maximum freedom in exploiting information resources.

The structure can be at various levels of completeness; at one extreme it can be developed to a full classification, as in the London Education Classification (Foskett & Foskett, 1974) or the English Electric Thesaurofacet (Aitchison *et al,* 1969), and at the other it can be left at broad subject groups. The two parts are usually linked by some kind of notation, which helps the user to move between the alphabetical list of terms and the classified arrangement. The main use of the classified arrangement is to give an overall picture of the subject area, and so help those who are trying to define an area they want to investigate, or those who want guidance to appropriate terms for questions they have already defined. Figure 5.2 shows an example of the relation between the alpha and classified listings from a thesaurus (Orna, 1978).

Figure 5.2 Relation between alpha and classified side of a thesaurus (from Engineering Industry Training Board thesaurus, 1978)

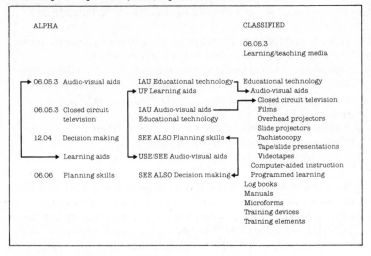

● When a thesaurus is necessary

The power and utility of a thesaurus have to be paid for; a good thesaurus takes a lot of time to compile. It is therefore necessary to be sure that the task is an absolutely essential one and that nothing else exists that will give the desired results, before embarking on it. The main factor in deciding is whether there is an existing recognized vocabulary for the subjects with which one is concerned. If there is, a thesaurus is almost certainly not needed; there will be comparatively few decisions to make, which can be easily recorded, and there will be a ready authority for reference. This is likely to be the case in scientific fields like zoology, geology and chemistry, which have their own well-established structure and vocabulary.

If, on the other hand, there is no recognized vocabulary and structure and the material cuts across many disciplines — as is the case with social history, anthropology and ethnography for instance — then it is likely to be necessary to establish some kind of control and to take a lot of decisions. In this situation, compiling a thesaurus may well be worth while. Figure 5.3 sets out in algorithm form some of the questions that need to be answered in deciding whether to embark on thesaurus construction.

Figure 5.3 Do I need to compile a thesaurus?

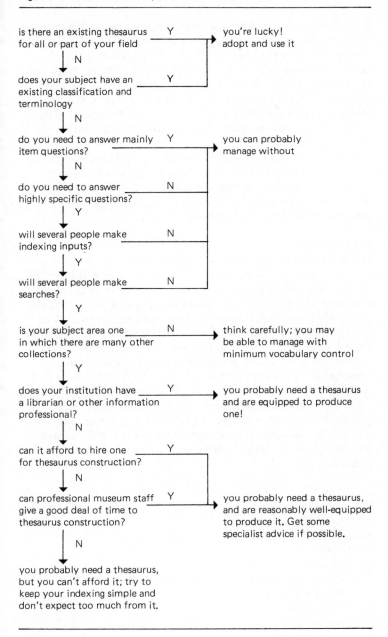

is there an existing thesaurus   Y   you're lucky!
for all or part of your field   adopt and use it
     N

does your subject have an   Y
existing classification and
terminology
     N

do you need to answer mainly   Y   you can probably
item questions?   manage without
     N

do you need to answer   N
highly specific questions?
     Y

will several people make   N
indexing inputs?
     Y

will several people make   N
searches?
     Y

is your subject area one   N   think carefully; you may
in which there are many other   be able to manage with
collections?   minimum vocabulary control
     Y

does your institution have   Y   you probably need a thesaurus
a librarian or other information   and are equipped to produce
professional?   one!
     N

can it afford to hire one   Y
for thesaurus construction?
     N

can professional museum staff   Y   you probably need a thesaurus,
give a good deal of time to   and are reasonably well-equipped
thesaurus construction?   to produce it. Get some
                            specialist advice if possible.
     N

you probably need a thesaurus,
but you can't afford it; try to
keep your indexing simple and
don't expect too much from it.

● Compiling a thesaurus

If the analysis of information problems suggests that a thesaurus is necessary, and the resources for compilation are available, there are certain practical steps which can help to keep the effort to a minimum while guaranteeing a reasonable result. The main principle for thesaurus construction can be expressed as 'Don't do it unless you have to, but if you must do it, make sure you do it well'. A good thesaurus is an invaluable aid and worth all the effort put into its construction; a bad one is a treacherous tool, and will never repay the time spent on it.

Thesaurus compilation can be a wholly manual task, or it can be done by computer, or it can be essentially manual but computer-assisted in some of the routine but vital operations. The principles can best be appreciated from a description of a wholly manual compilation, so that is discussed first.

● *Outline structure*
The first step is to decide on the categories of data for which standard terms are needed. An analysis like that shown in Figure 3.2 (p33) of the ways in to information which are likely to be needed, combined with a study of the data categories of the relevant MDA card if one exists, should help in establishing a working list which will make the structural framework of the thesaurus. This acts as an aide-memoire in thesaurus construction, and provides a ready-made location for terms as they are decided on. At the early stage of compilation the list of main categories can be quite flexible in both sequence and content; it is better not to be too hard and fast because experience will almost certainly make changes necessary. McInnes (1978) provides a good example of this stage for geology and minerals. She uses the data elements of the relevant MDA cards to provide data categories and a structure for them. For geology, the listing runs:

1   Form
2   Identification
2.1   Classified identification
2.2   Status
3   Collection
3.1   Place names/detail
3.2   Collection method
4   Acquisition
4.1   Acquisition method
5   Description
5.1   Condition

5.2   Part: Aspect: Description Keyword/Detail
5.2.1   Part
5.2.2   Aspect: Description
6   Process

It will be noted that these categories are not simply names of things; they also cover activities, like those listed under 'Process', and adjectives like those used to describe 'Condition'.

Since the most flexible way of building a thesaurus is to use a separate card for each term, it is helpful for a start to use each of the main categories as heading for a subject divider card. This makes it easy to file terms for the classified list as they are decided on. A5 (half the standard A4 paper size) is a good size for the purpose, as it allows plenty of working space.

It is as well not to attach notation (ie numerical or alpha-numeric coding) to the main categories as too early a stage, as it complicates the management of the inevitable second and third thoughts about sequence and structure.

● *Assembling terms*
The next stage consists of bringing together terms within the categories that have been established. Here it is possible to take either an 'encyclopaedic' approach — assembling a 'dictionary' for the given subject area before starting to index — or one based on the actual content of the collections. The latter uses only terms that relate to what is in the collections, and the vocabulary is built up as recording/indexing proceeds. This means that indexing and thesaurus construction can advance side by side, and so useful outputs can be obtained at an earlier stage than is possible if an exhaustive list is compiled before indexing starts. The problem of building a thesaurus while indexing is that the first inputs will be less well indexed than the later ones, but it is possible to overcome this by planning phased updating of earlier inputs so that they are ultimately brought up to the standard made possible by the fully developed thesaurus.

Various sources can be drawn on for vocabulary: standard glossaries or indexes, other thesauri (for example, the English Electric *Thesaurofacet* might well be used as a source for technological terms), standard reference works, the terminology that has already been used in recording, and current usage in the discipline concerned, as reflected in the periodical literature. McInness, in the article referred to earlier, describes the use of the Institute of Geological Sciences coding for rock names, and of keywords derived from the American Geological Institute glossary (Harrison & Sabine, 1972, and Gary, McAfee & Wolf, 1972), as the authority for terms used by the

Hunterian Museum for geology. Given the existence of such sources, it is not necessary in a subject field like geology to go further in thesaurus construction than a structured listing, drawing its terms from the chosen authority.

The compiler's knowledge of the subject and of the types of question that need answering can be put to good use in deciding where complex terms can be built up by co-ordinating simpler ones at the time of search, and where it is more appropriate to 'pre-coordinate' them — for example, should the concept 'Neolithic flint axes' be built up from the three separate terms 'Neolithic' 'Flint' and 'Axes' or should the terms be bound together into the three-word term 'Neolithic flint axes'? The answer will depend partly on the number of items involved, and partly on the possibilities for false co-ordination of separate terms (see Chapter 4, p52 and Chapter 9, p151 for example). Generally speaking, pre-coordination is indicated for concepts which are central to the collection and frequently sought.

● *Decisions on terms*
Where it is possible to use a printed source as the authority, problems of deciding on the standard term will not arise often. There will, however, need to be agreement among the people who assign index terms on the 'entry terms' that should be admitted. Such decisions can be reached either by discussion, or by making one person responsible for resolving the issue. In either case it is necessary to establish a procedure for bringing forward questions for decision and for recording the solution agreed on. This procedure will need to go on operating as a maintenance process once the thesaurus is in full operation. In fields where standard sources are lacking or cover only some categories of data, decision making is correspondingly more important, and it is essential to establish from the very beginning the procedures by which it will be handled, and to record them carefully (the subject of procedure manuals for information systems is discussed in Chapter 8 (pp 137—40).

● *Recording terms and instructions*
Recording must cover:
1) The standard index terms which it is decided to use, and the
   entry terms by which users may seek to access the information
2) Instructions and guidance on the use of terms.
It is essential to use a well-designed standard form for recording. Figure 5.4 shows an example used in constructing a thesaurus of education terms, and Figure 5.5 sets out the symbols commonly used in thesauri. The standard form makes it possible to build up for each term all the instructions and information that will be

Figure 5.4 Recording form for thesaurus terms

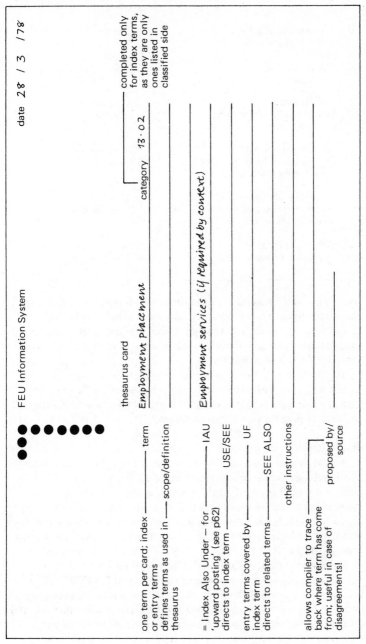

FEU Information System   date 28 / 3 /78

thesaurus card

category 13·02 ———— completed only for index terms, as they are only ones listed in classified side

Employment placement

Employment services (if required by context)

●●●●●●
●
●

one term per card; index ———— term
or entry terms
defines terms as used in —— scope/definition
thesaurus

= Index Also Under — for ———— IAU
'upward posting' (see p62)
directs to index term ———— USE/SEE

entry terms covered by ———— UF
index term

directs to related terms ———— SEE ALSO

other instructions

allows compiler to trace
back where term has come ┐ proposed by/
from; useful in case of ┘ source
disagreements!

69

Figure 5.5 Symbols most commonly used in thesauri

Symbol and meaning	Example
USE guides from entry to index term	Dess bed USE Folding bed
UF (Use for) shows entry terms covered by index term	Folding bed UF Dess bed
BT (Broader term) guides to more general index terms in same hierarchy	Folding bed BT Bed
NT (Narrower term) guides to more specific index terms in same hierarchy	Bed NT Folding bed
RT (Related term) guides to related terms	Divan RT Bed

needed in the final version of the thesaurus. It is possible to build the alphabetical and the classified listings simultaneously, if the cards can be photocopied. One set is filed alphabetically and the other by data category behind dividers labelled with the names of categories and sub-categories.

It is advisable to work for some time from the version on cards, until the rate of adding new terms has levelled off, as it will after a time. Producing a printed out list too early makes for difficulties because of insertions and transpositions.

● *The printed out version*
When the rate of addition has reached an acceptably low level it is possible to go over from cards to a more easily used printed out version of the thesaurus. At this stage, the notation for the main categories and sub-categories can be added to the cards for the index terms. It is advisable to accept that the first printed out version will still be susceptible to modification, and that a final one will not emerge till the draft has become dog-eared and much amended.

Using the thesaurus cards and following their instructions, it should be possible to produce an accurate typed listing of both alpha and classified sides, with all the necessary cross references between index and entry terms, etc in their proper place in the alpha list, and with narrower terms displayed under the broader terms to which they are subordinate in the classified side. Figure 5.6 shows an example from a thesaurus constructed without any mechanical aids and reproduced from a master copy typed on an ordinary manual typewriter.

● Mechanical aids

As a first step in mechanization, a word processor can be put to very good use in thesaurus construction and maintenance. The text can be held on magnetic tape, agreed changes can be printed out at frequent intervals, and a new version incorporating the changes — by means of the editing facility of the word processor — can be printed out whenever required.

If a computer is accessible, it can be used not only for updating as described above, but also for putting in and verifying the necessary complementary cross references, and for detecting errors and inconsistencies. If the thesaurus can be held on-line, interactive searches can be aided by display of relevant groups of terms on the VDU, so that the user is reminded of other possible approaches and can select different terms to modify his search strategy.

At the final level of mechanization, the task of compilation can be handled by the computer through a program which instructs it to print out the terms which have been used in the records, especially in 'natural language' descriptions (other than trivial and non-informative ones). The program can ensure that terms having the same root are brought together, regardless of the grammatical form in which they occur, or that pairs or clusters of terms which occur frequently in association are shown. Frequency of occurrence can also be shown. This permits a choice of terms to be made, and the process of generating the necessary cross references can then be carried out by the computer.

This is a brief outline of a subject on which there is quite an extensive literature. The interested reader is referred in particular to an excellent practical text by Aitchison & Gilchrist (1972), and to a theoretical study by Gilchrist (1971).

● Museum thesauri

Comparatively few thesauri have so far been compiled in the museum field. The best known is probably Chenhall's (1978), which is designed for dealing with man-made objects. It is limited as a retrieval tool because it is restricted to object names. There is, for example, no provision for materials, processes, operations, qualifying

Figure 5.6 Extracts from a manually constructed thesaurus
(from Engineering Industry Training Board thesaurus, 1978)

06.02	Implementation	use where report records implementation of recommendations IAU Benefits (if recorded)
	In-company training	USE/SEE Company training
18.08	In-house systems	
06.01.2	In-service training (training carried out while in employment, though not necessarily on the job)	
06.05.2	In-tray exercises	
13.07	Incentives	UF Bonuses Bonus schemes
03.02	Incomes	use only for incomes from <u>all</u> sources; otherwise USE/SEE Earnings <u>or</u> Pay SEE ALSO Pay administration

```
01
INTERNATIONAL RELATIONS

01.02
International relations

International

01.03
International organisations

Common Market
  Common Market budget
  Common Market information service
  Common Market institutions
  Common Market statistics
  European Social Fund
International organisations
International statistics

02
SOCIAL POLICY

02.01
Economic policy; Planning
```

adjectives, or place names, and this restricts its utility in dealing with man-made objects, where searches are often required for things made by a given process, or of a particular material, or originating from a specific place.

An archaeological thesaurus for Wessex Sites and Monuments Record (Rance *et al*) is in the process of compilation at the time of writing. The terms have been selected by curators in various museums, and the processing into a thesaurus is being carried out on the Hampshire County Council computer, using the local authority's software. The thesaurus is presented in three parts: an alpha listing of terms, a hierarchical presentation organized by subject area and displaying the relationships between terms, and an alpha list of key-words. Stone (1979) has also described the development of an archaeological thesaurus — this one arising from participation in a pilot project at St Albans Museum in the use of the MDA cards and GOS programs. A sophisticated model for thesaurus compilation as part of an overall computer system at the Hermitage in Leningrad is described by Sher (1978).

● Summary

Vocabulary control is necessary in order to:
— ensure consistency in terms so that everything relevant is retrieved
— guide users to the terms under which information is stored from other possible 'entry' terms
— make sure that users find information under terms which are at the level of precision they need
— help users who need a broader view

The most complete form of vocabulary control is a *thesaurus.*

A thesaurus is a *structured list* of terminology for a given subject area. It contains:
— *index terms* (which may be nouns, proper names, verbal nouns, or adjectives)
— *entry terms* which act a a lead to index terms
— *instructions and guidance*

The instructions:
— point the way from entry terms to index terms
— link specific terms with broader ones and vice versa
— relate terms to other relevant ones

The guidance:
– defines terms and indicates the scope of their usage in the thesaurus

Modern thesauri usually contain two listings of terms:
alphabetical and classified. The classified listing displays the structure
of the subject field and shows the hierarchical relationship between
terms.

Thesaurus construction is expensive in time and should be
undertaken only if:
1) There is no other available source of authority for vocabulary
2) There are adequate resources of time and skill for compiling.
A good thesaurus will repay all the effort put into construction;
a bad one is unsafe to use and the time devoted to it is pure waste.

Steps in thesaurus construction
|
develop outline structure of main categories
|
establish rules for compilation and decision-making procedures
|
decide on sources for terms
|
record terms on properly designed form
|
build alpha and classified lists simultaneously, using duplicate forms
|
produce draft printed out version when rate of addition of terms
has levelled out
|
add notation
|
produce final version
|
follow agreed maintenance and updating routines

Thesaurus construction can be entirely manual, or various levels of
machine aid can be used, ranging from word processor editing and
print out, through computer checking, updating and print out, to
computer compilation.

● References

Aitchison, J & Gilchrist, A *Thesaurus construction* Aslib, 1972

Aitchison, J, Gomersall, A & Ireland, R *Thesaurofacet: a thesaurus and faceted classification for engineering and related subjects* English Electric Company, 1969

Chenhall, R G *Nomenclature for museum cataloguing: a system for classifying man-made objects* Nashville, American Association for State and Local History, 1978

Foskett, D J and Foskett, J *The London education classification: a thesaurus/classification of English educational terms* Second edition, University of London Institute of Education, 1974

Gary, M, McAfee Jr, R & Wolf, C L (ed) *Glossary of geology* American Geological Institute, 1972

Gilchrist, A *The thesaurus in retrieval* Aslib, 1971

Harrison, R K & Sabine, P A *A petrological-mineralogical code for computer use* Report of the Institute of Geological Sciences No. 70/6, 1970

McInnes, C 'The Hunterian IRGMA geology vocabulary and grammar' *MDA information* 2(2) May 1978, 11–17

Orna, E *Engineering Industry Training Board thesaurus* Watford, Library and Information Services, Engineering Industry Training Board, 1978

Porter, M F 'Establishing a museum documentation system in the United Kingdom', *Museum* XXX(3/4) 1978, 169–78

Rance, A, Schadla-Hall, T & Magee, S V 'A thesaurus of archaeological terms for use with a sites and monuments record' (forthcoming)

Sher, J H 'The use of computers in museums: present situation and problems' *Museum* XXX(3/4) 1978, 132–8

Stone, S 'MDA user experience – St Albans Museums' *MDA information* 3(7) November 1979, 49–54

Chapter 6
Equipment for the job: the appropriate hardware for manual systems

This chapter is intended to help decision making on hardware for manual systems. Up to now, everything discussed has been relevant to both computer and manual systems. In discussing hardware — that is, the *physical means* in which information is stored and by which it is manipulated — the road has to branch. This chapter deals with manual systems, the next with computer systems. The branches re-unite in Chapter 8, which deals with manpower utilization, routines and procedures to make the best of whatever system and whatever combination of hardware and software is chosen. It is hoped that even readers firmly committed to computer use as the ultimate solution will look at the present chapter; it can often be instructive, as well as cheaper, to carry out trial and error essays with a manual system (especially if one lacks computer experience) and to get the 'bugs' out of that, before moving on to the more expensive investment and more costly correction of mistakes which are inevitable with computer use.

● Define the problem before buying a solution

The discussion of hardware has been deliberately left to this point. Unfortunately, consideration of information handling all too often starts from the hardware end instead of finishing there. People are sold the idea of edge-notched cards, optical coincidence cards, or computers, before they have analysed the nature of their problem, and then find themselves the owners of a solution and trying to fit their problem to it. In fact it is impossible to make a rational decision on the physical form in which records or indexes should be embodied, or on the physical means that should be used to manipulate and search the data, until we know clearly the purpose of the activity — who will use the data, what kinds of question they will seek to answer, and what types of output will be needed.

● Data vehicles

The pieces of material — paper, card, film or magnetic tape, for instance — that carry the data used in any system of information can be called 'data vehicles'. The terminology introduced in Chapters 3 and 4 (pp 35 and 48—51) to describe the two main types of question and the types of index used to answer them — *item* and *feature* — can also be applied to data vehicles. An item vehicle carries full details of a given item; a feature vehicle carries the name of a feature and the identification of items which possess that feature (the amount of information can range from just the record numbers to the full record, via selected extracts from the record). For manual systems, the choice normally lies among various types of card, as described below.

● *Plain item cards*
These are cards without any pre-printing, which carry the details of the item in some standard sequence, and are arranged in a sequence that derives from some chosen characteristic of the item. The typical form of arrangement for item cards is by item name or number. Item cards can also be arranged according to other characteristics, for example by classification category. A classified catalogue is in effect an item index arranged according to features. Figure 6.1 shows a typical plain item card.

● *Plain feature cards*
If plain cards are used for features they are headed with the name of a feature, and carry some identification for one or more items having that feature. Figure 6.2 shows an example. These are either arranged in a single alpha sequence by name of feature or grouped according to particular kinds of feature — for example place names, materials, processes, etc — into a number of separate alpha sequences.

● *Pre-printed item cards*
These are item cards with the data categories preprinted on them so that information can be entered in a standard format. The MDA cards are an example. They can be replicated in whole or in part to produce item or feature indexes, as described in the introduction to the IRGMA documentation system (Roberts 1976, p10): 'the description associated with each heading may be all or part of the record from which the heading is extracted. It may vary from a maximum (all the record) to a minimum (the identity number of the record and thing).'

Figure 6.1 Plain item card

Title	Ship model 'John Bowes'
Provenance & description	Contemporary model of iron collier built 1852 at Newcastle on Tyne by General Iron Screw Collier Company (Charles & George Palmer)
Bibliographic reference	Atkinson, F Industrial archaeology of North-East England. David & Charles 1974 pp 159–60
Size	Overall length 27 inches
Donor	Mr J Sanderson
Date	15 3 1972
Reference no.	S108

Figure 6.2 Plain feature card, from a topographical index to a picuture collection

NORWICH
   Fye Bridge
   W C J Thirtle
   1352.E.235.951

● *Pre-printed feature cards*

These are variously called uniterm or ten-column cards. Like plain feature cards they are headed with the name of a feature, but the identifying numbers of items having the feature are arranged in columns according to their last digit (this is just to gain a better scatter of numbers, which aids the comparisons between cards which are an essential part of the search procedure). Searches are made by taking out the cards with the required feature names on them, comparing the numbers on them, and finding those that appear on all the cards. By definition, the items having those numbers will possess the required combination of features. Figure 6.3 shows an example of a search carried out with ten-column cards.

● *Edge-notched item cards*

These cards are designed to make it possible to use an item index for both item and feature searches. It will be remembered that normally the answering of a feature question from an item index entails scanning each record to see if it has the desired feature or features. This difficulty is overcome in an ingenious way with the edge-notched card. It has numbered and lettered holes round its edges which, individually, or in agreed combinations, can be used to represent features. The middle of the card carries a description of the item. If the item possesses a given feature, the hole or holes standing for that feature are clipped to make open notches. Searches are carried out by 'needling' the pack of cards. If we are looking for a given feature, the needle is put through the appropriate hole in the pack. Since the items possessing the feature have that hole clipped, those cards will fall back into the container which houses the cards when the pack is lifted on the needle. It is possible to search for combined features by using more than one needle. Foskett (1970) gives a description of the use of these cards and of coding to allow multiple use of the holes. Their limitation is that, even using combinations of holes, only a comparatively small number of features can be provided for. Figure 6.4 shows an example.

● *Punched feature cards*

The usual term for these is optical coincidence cards, though they are sometimes found masquerading coyly under the name of peek-a-boo cards. They are a sophisticated version of the ten-column cards described above, carrying a network of printed numbered positions, arranged in squares (usually 100 to a square, arranged in smaller squares of 25). The identifying numbers of items that possess a given feature are punched out to make a hole (corresponding to writing the numbers on a ten-column card). The comparison needed for searches is done by superimposing the feature cards over a light

Figure 6.3 Pre-printed feature cards
Using 10-column cards for co-ordinate search

Search query
Dresses made of Jacquard weave brocade

Query translated into index terms
1 Jacquard weave
2 Brocade
3 Dresses

Search method
1 Extract feature cards headed with these index terms
2 Note numbers common to all three
These represent the items which meet the search criteria, in this case items 1570 and 1895

JACQUARD WEAVE

0	1	2	3	4	5	6	7	8	9
(1570)			1893	2254	(1895)	1916		3068	
2130									

BROCADE

0	1	2	3	4	5	6	7	8	9
(1570)					(1895)	1916		2368	2409
2430	2431	2432	2433	2434	2435	2436	2437	2438	2439
2450	2441	2442	2443	2444	2445	2446	2447	2448	2449
								3068	

DRESSES

0	1	2	3	4	5	6	7	8	9
910	911	912	913	914	905	906	907	908	909
920	921	922	923	924	915	916	917	918	919
930	931	932	933	934	925	926	927	928	929
1060	1061	1062	1903	1054	1055	1056	1057	1058	1059
(1570)	1901	1902		1894	(1895)	1896	1897	1898	1899
1900				1904	1905	1906	1907	1908	1909
1910									

Figure 6.4 Edge punched card used to make feature index for objects found on archaeological sites

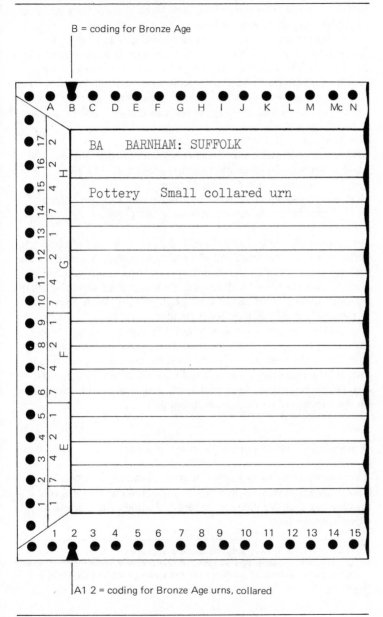

B = coding for Bronze Age

BA   BARNHAM: SUFFOLK

Pottery   Small collared urn

A1 2 = coding for Bronze Age urns, collared

Reproduced by courtesy of the Castle Museum, Norwich

source. The numbers* which are present on all the cards show as spots where the light shines straight through holes which coincide with one another. Optical coincidence cards are stored in deep 'tubs' and need a light box and some kind of hand or mechanical punch.

Besides the type of search illustrated in Figure 6.3, which is interested only in items that have all three named features and rejects those which have only two of them, it is possible to perform other logical operations with optical coincidence or ten-column cards. One can also search for items which possess either one feature or another feature, or the two combined; and one can specify features that are *not* wanted.

The three types of operation are usually called:

AND — records which contain given features in combination

OR — records which contain either a combination of given features or one or other of them

NOT — records which contain certain features, excluding those where certain other features are also present.

Ten-column and optical coincidence cards allow them to be performed in a very direct and comprehensible way. A computer can perform them much quicker but the essential process is still one of comparison. The use of feature cards for co-ordinate searching almost demands some kind of agreed vocabulary, with guidance about the terms which should be used for particular concepts, especially in the cases where it has been decided to build up complex concepts by combining two or more simple ones. Without agreed terms and guidance in their use, much of the power of co-ordinate searches is lost and the process becomes hit and miss — a point perhaps not always appreciated by those who invest in optical coincidence systems on the strength of hardware sales promotion.

● Relating system requirements to equipment

It is possible to draw up a simple matrix, as shown in Figure 6.5, to help relate the system requirements to the available options; this makes a basis for deciding on the range of equipment that merits closer consideration.

---

*With optical coincidence cards *it is essential to use a simple number, unique to the item;*alpha-numeric codes cannot be used. With ten-column cards, so long as the number is unique, it can be of any form, though other things being equal, simplest is best.

Figure 6.5 Deciding the form of index to meet your needs

	Plain item (A)	Plain feature (B)	Punched item (C)	Punched feature (D)	A + B (E)	A + D (F)	C + D (G)
1 Single item questions	●						
2 Single feature and combined feature questions. Small collection		●					
3 Single and combined item questions + some feature questions. Not many features needed			●				
4 Single and combined feature questions, mainly combined; medium to large collection				●			
5 Both item and feature questions; small collection					●		
6 Mainly feature + some item questions: medium to large collection						●	
7 Both item and feature questions; medium to large collection. Part of it needs mainly item questions + quick answers to questions on single features; rest mainly feature questions.							●

In most situations, it is helpful to use more than one type of data vehicle. This gives flexibility and allows for meeting different types of requirement in the most simple way. The idea of conjugate indexes, which complement one another by allowing for different ways in to the data, has already been mentioned in Chapter 4 (p51). It is often helpful to use two different types of data vehicle to achieve a conjugate index.

If punched feature cards are used, it is economic to keep them for subject-type features (eg object names, materials, processes, etc) and to use either plain or ten-column feature cards for such things as names of persons, firms, or organizations which are associated with objects. This is more economic, because in the nature of things there are likely to be comparatively few items associated with any one individual, firm or organization, and so it is wasteful to devote a whole 10,000-position card to terms that will be used infrequently. There are techniques (described in Jolley, 1968) for using codes to represent names which allow two or three punched feature cards to be used in conjunction to represent a large number of names, but this seems misplaced ingenuity, as it involves an extra look-up operation to find the right code, and the possibilities of error are great. The use of 10-column cards for 'identifiers' like proper names of people and institutions makes it easy to carry out co-ordinate searches involving names as well as subject features.

Where donor indexes are concerned, it is obviously necessary to have a plain item card index, carrying the name, address and details of donated items.

In some situations, it is also helpful to maintain two or more banks of the same kind of data vehicle; for example, separate sets of optical coincidence cards for different collections whose use does not overlap to any significant extent.

A good example of a manual system which uses a variety of inter-related card indexes, feature and item, pre-printed and plain, is described in Chapter 9 (pp 143—4).

In deciding the extent to which multiple indexes should be used, judgement is required. The guiding principle is to use whatever combination makes it easy to carry out the searches which are essential, to start no indexes which do not repay the effort of compiling, and *maintain scrupulously any indexes that are set up.* It is also very desirable to use the same terminology throughout, whatever the physical form of index. Having to search a number of different indexes sequentially is no great hardship as long as one is using the same search terms on each; it becomes very laborious, however, if one has to remember to use different vocabularies for each index. As mentioned in Chapter 5 (p59), it is one of the ways in which a thesaurus can be useful — as a unifying device to link a number of different physical means of holding data.

● Microforms

Just as many public and academic library catalogues are nowadays
held on roll microfilm or on the postcard-sized sheets of microfilm
called microfiche, it is equally possible to use microforms as a data
vehicle in museum systems — both manual and computerized. Their
advantages lie in space saving, security, and the possibility of
distributing to users within or outside the institutions. The easiest
and most obvious applications are for plain item or feature cards and
for pre-printed item cards, because these are used by locating the
desired place in the file and reading the relevant cards, and it is easy
to key film or fiche to aid location. For uses which involve locating
and comparing two or more cards — as with edge-notched item and
pre-printed or punched feature cards — microform is not suitable,
because its essence is the putting of many discrete records on to a
single record, which defeats the object of retrieval methods that
involve comparisons. It is, however, possible to use microforms for
the master records to which indexes used for post-coordinate search
relate.

Microfiche, or fiche jackets (that is, fiche-sized transparent holders
into which strips of 16mm microfilm can be fed by machine to make
up a fiche), is the most suitable material for holding records whose
originals are separate cards. Duplicates can be made quickly and
quite cheaply on the spot, with a diazo duplicator, and efficient and
portable fiche readers are not too costly. The best source of advice
is the National Reprographic Centre for Documentation, which
publishes evaluations of equipment and abstracts of relevant books
and articles in its journal *Reprographics quarterly*. Some applications
of microforms in museums are described in Chapter 9.

● Word processing

The most usual way of entering data on to data vehicles in manual
systems is possibly still hand writing, with typing on a manual or
electric typewriter a close second. In both cases, the main difficulties
lie in correcting records and in replicating them. Photocopying
has improved the situation greatly, but the photocopier can only
reproduce an exact duplicate; it allows no format variation. The
recent advent of the word processor opens up interesting possibilities
for those whose business is the creation, replication and manipulation
of records of data. In essence, the word processor is a typewriter
which, besides originating hard copy as the keys are struck, can
simultaneously store the data on magnetic tape or disc. The
electronically stored data can be edited, corrected, added to and

subtracted from without large-scale re-typing. The data held in the typewriter's 'memory' can be printed out at will, either in the format in which they were input, or with variations. The extent of the variation in format which is possible depends on the degree of sophistication of the machine.

If access to a word processor is a possibility, it is well worth thinking about how its potential might be exploited. One example of a pioneering and well thought out use of a word processor is described in Chapter 9 (pp 154–5). The National Reprographic Centre for documentation has a grant from the British Library to study the application of word processors in specialized information centres, and acts an an informal clearinghouse for information about developments in this field.

● Sources of advice

In making decisions on whether to invest in hardware, it is a sound idea not to be guided solely by what the salesman or the promotional literature says. If one is thinking of buying a particular kind of equipment for a given job, it is invaluable to go and see it in operation for a similar purpose, and to talk to people who have already invested in it. They will be able to demonstrate the ways they have discovered of exploiting the equipment, and will also be able to reveal any snags they have met. Reputable firms are usually willing to put potential buyers in touch with people already using their product.

● Summary

Analysis of information problems and needs must precede decisions on hardware.

The main data vehicles for manual systems are cards of various kinds:

item	*feature*
1) plain	4) plain
2) pre-printed	5) pre-printed (ten-column)
3) edge-notched	6) punched (optical coincidence)

AND, OR and NOT logical operations can be carried out with 3), 5), & 6). An agreed vocabulary is highly desirable, particularly for post-coordinate searching with feature cards.

It is usually helpful to use more than one type of data vehicle to meet various needs. Use whatever combination facilitates essential searches, and use the same terminology for all types of index employed in a system.

Plain item and feature cards and pre-printed item cards can be microfilmed. Fiche or jacketed fiche is the most useful form of microform for the purpose.

Word processors can be used to aid the editing and replication of records in a variety of formats from a single output.

● References

Foskett, A C *A guide to personal indexes using edge-notched, uniterm and peek-a-boo cards* Second edition Bingley. 1970

Jolley, J L *Data study* World University Library. Weidenfeld & Nicolson. 1968

Roberts, D A *Introduction to the IRGMA documentation system* Part 1 IRGMA. 1976

National Reprographic Centre for documentation
Hatfield Polytechnic
Endymion Road Annexe
Hatfield
Herts
AL10 8AU

Chapter 7
Factors in the management of museum computer systems*

The potential of computers for helping museums to achieve active
and economic use of their collections has already been touched on
in this book, and will be examined in more detail in this chapter; in
summary the principal advantages are:
— Interfiling new records can be done easily and with fewer errors
than in a manual system.
— Information can be updated on all relevant records by a single
command.
— Post-coordinate indexing of records is simple, and fresh indexes
automatically reflect any recent changes in the main file of records.
— Records may be selected and retrieved according to many
combinations of required data, and error-free transcription of
retrieved records is automatic.

A good review of reasons in favour of museum computerization
is given in Gautier (1978).

Computerization can also afford opportunites for inter-museum
cooperation, for example in the collaborative regional Collection
Research Units currently operating in the UK (Hancock and Pettitt,
1980).

Having made the primary decision to computerize, however, the
museum authorities are then faced with a range of subsidiary
decisions on two levels. First must be chosen what to computerize
and why, which machine to use, what programs to run, what staff to
involve and, above all, how much money to spend. These decisions
would normally be the province of the museum management
committee, with expert advice from suitably qualified staff or from
outside consultants; guidance on this phase is presented in the first
half of the chapter, 'Groundwork'. The second-level, or operational,
decisions should then be taken by a specially convened computer
committee chaired by the System Manager; guidance on the various
stages to be considered is given in the second half of the chapter,
'Organizing the system'.

It should be realized that, although much more complex, in
essence a computerized data handling system is identical to a manual
system. Each contains three basic elements, *hardware*, *software* and

---

* Contributed by Charles Pettitt, Manchester Museum

people (sometimes rather chillingly termed *liveware*). In a manual system, the recording medium (file or edge-punched cards, etc) and its container (filing cabinets, folders) are the *hardware;* the *software* consists of the labelled boxes on the card, the file dividing markers, and the instruction manuals; the people usually consist of curators with technical or secretarial help. The essential difference between computerized and manual systems is that in the latter the *processing power* to order, sort and retrieve the information is provided by a human brain, while in a computerized system these tasks are done by the *central processing unit* (or CPU) of the computer. In human terms, though, a computer is fast, accurate and very, very stupid, and it must never be overlooked that it is *people* who create, develop, maintain and operate a computer system.

In both types of system the three elements are welded together by an overall strategy, but because of the complex interactions involved in computerized data processing it is vital that an integrated system approach is taken. A system, once started, rapidly gains momentum and inertia, and making significant changes such as introducing a new facility can prove troublesome and expensive. Therefore time spent trying to work out the 'system concepts' at the beginning is rarely wasted. A system that is allowed to grow like Topsy is likely to end up all Topsy Turvey! Mumford and Henshall (1978) deal in detail with this aspect of the work.

● Groundwork

● *First steps*
The most important first steps in a computerization programme are to examine available resources and needs, and to define the objectives of the system.

— What resources are available? ie staff with knowledge or experience of computers, access to data preparation or computer processing facilities, access to advice on museum computerization. If little or no experience is available it is strongly recommended that a small pilot scheme be tried before commitment is made on a large scale, for nothing can replace first-hand experience in assessing both the potential and the problems of computerization.
— Why is it being done? Typical reasons, and some of their implications are:
To save money. Applies only if the museum already spends significant amounts of money on catalogue production.

To gain kudos. If so, output formats will be important, especially microfiche and computer typesetting facilities; upper and lower case output will be essential.

To assist answering inquiries. Good information retrieval routines will be necessary, possibly *interactive* working will be required.

To provide specialized reports. The correct range of input must be provided, eg valuations if insurance inventories are needed, special grid references for planning departments, etc.

To make better use of curatorial staff time. Special input documents can reduce time spent accessioning, or on loan management. By examining working practices, non-curatorial tasks can be identified and transferred to non-specialists. Ability to print out labels automatically can be an advantage.

To aid internal research. More direct staff access to the computer may be needed, ie more terminals provided. Standard statistics and graphics packages should also be made available, and the cataloguing package provide suitable input to such other packages.

To assist display or conservation. Ease of update will be needed.

To help with administration. Special facilities may need building into the system: payroll, accounts and address file programs, for example, which will not be covered by the cataloguing package.

— What general strategy should be adopted?
At first sight the work involved in computer-aided cataloguing will seem extremely daunting for most museums. A useful general strategy is to start by planning the computerization of all new accessions from some convenient date in the near future. This then limits the remaining problem to the backlog of material acquired before that date, which, although probably enormous, is now at least *finite* and not ever-increasing.

— Which sections of the museum are to be involved in providing input?
Collection departments. For new accessions all departments should be included; when dealing with the backlog, the management must decide whether to instruct all departments to identify suitable subjects for computerization, or whether involvement is to be voluntary.

Non-collection departments. Conservation, display and administration might all benefit from the application of computer techniques.

It is very important that *all* the staff members likely to be affected by the computer proposal are involved in the discussions as early as possible. This will not only help to allay fears and suspicions, but will highlight any particular problems individual departments might face.

90

— How much money will be made available? In most institutions, the most difficult question of all! However, the answer to this and all other questions must be known before a sensible choice can be made of hardware and software, and the planning of the system can begin. Don't rush this stage; listen to all the advice that can be obtained and examine all the options.

● *Hardware*
The pieces of electronic and electro-mechanical equipment that make up the tangible part of a computing installation are known collectively as *hardware*. A museum that wants to computerize its records obviously must obtain access to suitable hardware, and there are three ways in which this may be achieved.
1) The museum may install its own computer facility.
2) It may obtain on-line access to a large time-sharing computer (a *main-frame*) elsewhere.
3) It may send all its records away to be processed by a bureau service.

The options are not mutually exclusive, for example a museum might contract out its data preparation (see page 110) to a bureau while doing all its processing via on-line terminals to the mainframe installation of the local government authority to which it belongs.

A museum-owned installation
With the current widespread advertizing of very low price micro- and mini-computers this option can seem attractive at first sight. However it must be remembered that even a small museum will generate a significant quantity of data and that even with add-on storage on *floppy discs* the capacity of a micro-computer will be limited compared to that of a large mainframe or mini-computer. Although processing power is now becoming very cheap, to give satisfactory results an installation also requires considerable on- and off-line storage, and a range of input and output peripherals, such as card or disc readers, magnetic tape reel or cassette decks, and printers. Even buying the smallest and cheapest equipment on the market the total cost of a complete installation will run into several thousand pounds. It must be realised that much of this cheaper equipment is designed for low-volume domestic or office use; a small portable printer, for example, will soon fail if made to hammer out long files for hours on end. On the other hand, unless the equipment is going to be intensively used it is not very cost-effective for a museum to tie up scarce capital in this way. The cost of maintaining all this equipment is usually not slight and, in the light of the present rapid advance of technology, it could become obsolete very swiftly.

Another drawback to this approach is the significant delay that can be caused by the slow processing of large files, during which time the machine usually cannot handle any other work such as input, output or retrieval. A thousand 300-character records on a floppy disc may take several minutes to sort into a new order using a large word-processor type micro-computer; the same job on a large mainframe would take less than 10 seconds.

Access to a time-sharing mainframe or using a bureau

In the present writer's opinion, therefore, most museums would be well advised to choose options 2) or 3) above, certainly until they have acquired considerable experience. The only exception is likely to be the very large museum that can afford to set up a comprehensive computing department, such as those run by the British Museum and the Natural History Museum in London; although even those institutions make use of computing power elsewhere to back up their own machines. Any museum with its own computer will have to acquire the necessary skilled staff to operate the machines, and this chapter is not intended as a manual for such organizations. Thus the guidance given from now on will be aimed at helping museums obtain the maximum returns from options 2) and 3); a detailed account of the operation of a medium-sized museum computing facility will be found in McAllister (1978). By going to a bureau or by arranging access to a timesharing mainframe a museum will at one stroke avoid heavy capital outlay *and* obtain considerable expert back-up which could prove invaluable when setting up the scheme.

Micro-computers do have a place in museums, however, either as 'intelligent' terminals connected to the distant mainframe, or for some basic administrative functions such as address lists and accounts, or as an integral part of a gallery display. Their usefulness to curators for academic research calculations is doubtful; any problem that cannot be solved on a good programmable pocket calculator is probably better run on the mainframe using the sophisticated statistics and graphics packages that should be available.

Choice of installation

When attempting to choose the installation to use, the following questions should be asked
— Cost. Ideally, free processing will be arranged via the organization responsible for the management of the museum (eg a university or a local council). If this cannot be so, try to arrange for an annual payment to cover a given allocation of computer resources. If a charge is to be made according to work done, try to obtain firm figures — if possible run test jobs as 'benchmarks' to establish the

cost objectively. Can costs be reduced by running jobs at low priority, eg overnight?

— Ease of access. Other things being equal the nearer the mainframe or bureau, the better, for this reduces transport costs of data-tapes, cards and listings, and also line rental charges for any on-line terminal in the museum. Trouble-shooting is also simpler if museum and computing staff can meet easily to discuss problems.

— Facilities available. Does the machine under consideration support the chosen *software*? If not, what would it cost to *implement* it there, and who would then be responsible for maintaining it? Can the installation provide output in the forms and to the quality required?

— Service. Can 'turn-around' be guaranteed? Are the times quoted satisfactory? Can costs be reduced by accepting a slower turn-around? If *on-line* access is provided, for how many hours a day? Is access permitted in the evenings and at the weekends? What advisory service is offered?

— Security. Are the system safeguards and reporting facilities adequate? Is the service well established and, if it should close down, how easy will it be to transfer to another installation?

Wherever possible, contact other museums already using the service under consideration, and obtain their views. It is as well always to insist on a trial period before signing any formal contract, particularly in order to establish *actual* as opposed to *estimated* charges.

If a museum has no obvious access to computer facilities, before going to the expense of a commercial or semi-commercial bureau, investigate local industry. In terms of the computer power available within a large industrial concern, the amount of resources needed by a museum is trivial and such concerns may well be prepared to offer free or heavily subsidized computing to 'their' local museum as a public relations exercise.

Finally, with time-sharing machines, do you want to operate in *batch mode* or *interactively?* The former implies putting a batch of records into the system, processing them in some way, and obtaining the results as output; once the job is running there is no way of altering the instructions to the machine nor of keeping track of what is happening to the data. In an *interactive* system the machine can be made to report back at intervals and to accept new data or new instructions given according to the contents of the reports. This method permits the user to make choices between possible operations while the job is running.

A machine designed for batch operation cannot usually be made interactive, although an interactive machine usually can run in batch mode. Interactive working is useful mainly in development work and for the on-line retrieval of information; the production of catalogues and indexes may be handled satisfactorily in batch mode.

● *Software*
Software is the collective term for computer instructions; it includes both the written-out programs (called *source-listings*) and the *machine-readable* version. Other software includes *compilers* to translate source-listings into the internal language of the machine, *operating systems* which enable the machine to organize its work efficiently, and *manuals* to tell humans how to operate it all.

In practice, the only piece of *software* a museum needs to decide upon is the group of programs it is going to use to manipulate its data. Such a group of programs is called a *processing package.*

The package will usually be written in a high-level *computer language* such as FORTRAN or BCPL. If the language is not already available on the chosen machine, before the package can work, the machine will need to possess a compiler for that language.

The basic operations to be done on museum data are few; sort records into order according to some rule (eg alphabetic order or numeric order), merge in new records to the file, correct and update records already present, select records from the file according to given criteria, printout the records or parts of them. In computing terms these operations are all relatively simple, although the sheer volume of the data usually puts a premium on efficiency in the programs used, if processing time is to be kept reasonably short (and costs kept down).

Several suitable packages are already widely available, either free or at a cost far below that likely to be incurred in writing anything comparable locally. It is strongly recommended that an 'off-the-peg' package is used if at all possible, because organizing the computerization of a musum's data is complicated enough without adding the tedious business of *de-bugging* (correcting errors in) a new set of programs. The 'commercial' programs mostly have been thoroughly tested by numerous users, and reliable results should be obtained quickly from a new *implementation.* Once a package is running, however, useful local enhancements may be quite feasible. If one exists, the *user group* for the chosen package should be joined, as the contacts made can provide much helpful advice should things go wrong.

Packages

Typical packages suitable for museum work include the following:
— FAMULUS. Written in the widely available language FORTRAN.
Created at the Pacific South West Forest and Range Experimental
Station (California) of the US Department of Agriculture in 1969
and now available free. Numerous implementations world-wide; in
the UK has been considerably enhanced at the University of
Manchester Regional Computer Centre and is in use by Manchester
Museum. Batch mode operation only, input and output formats
restricted. FAMULUS is the Latin name for an alchemist's assistant.
— GOS. Written in the language BCPL. Created by Dr M Porter
(after Dr J Cutbill) 1976-78 at the MDAU, Duxford, near
Cambridge, UK. Cost to museums £500 — £1000 per implementation
(more to commercial organizations). Implemented on mainframes at
Cambridge and Manchester Universities and on mini-computers at
the British Museum and the National Maritime Museum, London.
Designed to cope with museum records of any complexity. Batch
mode operation only, input and output formats largely unrestricted.
The name GOS is not an acronym and has no deeper meaning.
— GRIPHOS. Written in the language PL1 (which is available only
on IBM machines). Developed by the Museum Computer Network
in US and implemented at several American sites. Batch mode
package. GRIPHOS stands for General Retrieval of Information and
Processing for the Humanity Oriented Sciences.
— SPIRES. Also written in PL1. Developed and currently maintained
by members of the Data Base Systems Group, Stanford Centre for
Information Processing (SCIP). Implemented at several North
American sites and at Newcastle University in the UK, where it is in
use by the Hancock Museum. Interactive package. SPIRES is an
acronym for the Stanford Public Information Retrieval System.

Several other packages have been successfully used by museums,
such as G-EXEC (similar to SPIRES), GIPSY and SELGEM; details
of the suppliers of some other packages are given on p184.

Even if the decision has been pre-empted somewhat by the
availability of one or other package at the chosen processing site, it
is advisable to obtain and read the manuals of as many as possible
of the above packages, for this will give a good background
knowledge of their relative strengths and complexities.

Ease of use may also be an important aspect of a package's
suitability. FAMULUS and SPIRES, for example, are both user-
oriented, and can be operated by a small set of simple commands.
The basic GOS package, however, requires considerable expertise
to run, although the application package currently being written
by the MDAU staff will make this package much simpler to operate.

Before finally settling upon the package to be used, try and visit an institution that is already using the package, to get first-hand experience of its capabilities. Make sure it gives the results you require, and try to discover how many other museums are also using the package in your area.

Maintenance
Once the package is running satisfactorily it will still require maintenance. Unexpected *bugs* may occur when you apply a new type of data, or some change in the *operating system* of the computer used may cause the package to give strange results or even to fail totally. Correcting such faults requires an experienced programmer, and ideally software maintenance should be the responsibility of the staff at the computer installation. If the package has been especially implemented for a museum, however, the cost of maintenance may well be charged to the museum and an annual allocation of funds will be necessary for this. All changes to the package must be rigorously documented, as must all local enhancements made.

● *People*
People are the most important part of the system, and the advice given in chapter 8 should be studied carefully in the planning stages. A computerization project that fails to get the support of the relevant curators, and for which insufficient expertise is available locally, would be better abandoned, or at most run as a small pilot project.

Any museum computerization programme must employ people in a number of roles, as curator, cataloguer, data preparation operator, computer operator, programmer and system manager.

In a very small museum the single resident professional could well combine the first two roles, with all the remaining jobs being contracted out to a bureau service such as that offered in the UK by the MDAU. At the other end of the scale a large national museum with its own computer unit may employ several people for each job, except that of system manager. The responsibilities of this latter post must always be undivided, and discharged by a single person albeit with deputies and/or assistants. The system manager is the lynchpin of the whole operation, and the correct choice for this post is the most crucial one for the whole project.

When planning the project it will be necessary to assign the staff involved to each role, to employ new staff for certain jobs (eg cataloguers), or to decide what work to contract out. One member of staff may have to assume more than one role, eg a curator may have to double as system manager. Whenever possible the system manager post should not be contracted out but filled from within the museum.

The curator, being an expert in the subject matter of the collections in his or her charge, will be responsible for the academic input to the operation. Guided by curators, the cataloguers capture the data and complete the data input sheets; they may also be subject specialists. In Manchester Museum it has been found that because of the degree of qualitative judgement involved in cataloguing geological and archaeological objects, cataloguers must be subject specialists; for natural history, however, non-specialists can provide very good cataloguers and lack of a scientific training is no handicap at all.

When organizing the system do not forget visiting scholars and volunteer workers, for they too can provide substantial input. Indeed, computerization often affords a method of making the work of volunteers in particular more rewarding for the individual and for the institution.

The data preparation operator converts the data into machine readable form; where multiple on-line terminals are available cataloguers can fulfil this function also by typing the data straight into the machine, perhaps without first completing a data input sheet. Such a state of affairs is unlikely to exist in many museums, however, and the services of data prep operators will be required.

Using a bureau service or distant time-sharing mainframe almost certainly means the computer operator and programmer jobs will be contracted out. The former actually pushes the buttons and flicks the switches to make the computer work; storing and mounting magnetic tapes, operating the system dumper and trouble-shooting hardware faults also come under the heading of 'operating'. The programmers, backed by a systems analyst, look after the software, eliminating bugs and adding enhancements as required.

The system manager oversees the whole operation; it is his or her task to see that the work flows smoothly, that targets and deadlines are met and that the end product is of the quality required. It is best if the system manager is a museum-trained person with a knowledge of computers. If because of lack of internal expertise a museum decides to strengthen the team by appointing a computer specialist, or an information scientist, without museum experience, it is strongly advised that one of the curatorial staff be made system manager and the new appointee is made his or her assistant. Such an arrangement is not only reassuring to the other curators involved but should also ensure the operational system is tailored to suit the museum's requirements and not *vice versa.*

An alternative to hiring computer expertise is to arrange for an existing member of staff to receive additional training in computing. Cataloguers may need some training in the use of on-line terminals for editing, and in the use of the adopted data standards; curators also will need some educating in the philosophy of electronic data processing, and internal training will normally be the responsibility of the system manager.

Nowadays people are a very expensive resource so they should be used intelligently. The computerization system should be designed to amplify the talents of staff, not to stifle them and turn them into machine-minders. Remember the means are not the ends, for computing *per se*, being new and exciting, can often threaten to overshadow the primary purpose of the project, which should be to increase the availability of the data inherent in the museum collections.

Before starting to plan the detailed organization of the system, one last decision is needed, the number of man years to be available for the project, and possibly the time span of the first phase of the work, upon which the decision to go further will be based. The critical work time will probably be that of curators and cataloguers, for their commitment will govern the needs of the rest of the operation.

● Organizing the system

Once the management decisions have been taken, it falls to the system manager to oversee planning of the operational details of the scheme within the guide-lines set. The work will involve constant discussions with management, curators and computing staff, both informally and within a series of sub-committees. In addition the system manager will now need to become completely familiar with the intricacy of the chosen *software package*, and with any *hardware* constraints that apply. He should also try to gain a user's knowledge of the *operating system* and the *system editor* on the machine to be used.

The overall progress of the scheme should be reported back at intervals, either to a specially convened 'computer committee' or, with less fuss, as an agenda item at any regular management meeting.

The various stages through which information passes may be categorized as:
1) data capture
2) data preparation and input
3) data processing, error checking and data storage
4) output

The organization of each stage is dealt with in detail below; monitoring will be necessary at all the above stages and is treated separately at the end of the chapter.

The system manager should now construct a work flow diagram of the proposed system; Figure 7.1 shows such a diagram of a typical computerized information system. The flow diagram is an invaluable aid to planning, and will also help in explaining the proposed system to curators. Manual catalogues and indexes are familiar to museum staff and most would profess to understand how such systems work but, despite its underlying similarity, psychologically a computer based system is likely to seem alien to the same staff.

Therefore the *user-interface*, ie the parts of the system seen by a curator, should be as simple and easily understood as possible. While there should be no need for a curator to 'learn computing' the system manager should spare no efforts to make the curators aware of the potential of the system, in particular its advantages over any existing manual system.

Once enthusiasm is aroused, however, great care must be taken not to foster unrealistic expectations. In the early stages curators' attitudes will tend to range from dismissive to the attribution of totally unrealizable abilities to the computer, and a single curator may well fluctuate rapidly from one extreme to the other and back again with each small success or failure of the developing system. Coping with these attitudes calls for a great deal of patient diplomacy on the part of the system manager, and to succeed he must himself be imbued with an unshakeable faith in the system he is creating.

● *Compiling the work schedule*
The next major task of the system manager will be to compile the work schedule that will set out precisely which objects are to be catalogued during the first phase of the scheme.

Curatorial staff should be asked to say which parts of the collections in their care they want to have included in the cataloguing programme. If more than a pilot scheme is envisaged it is best to adopt a 'project' approach. In consultation with the curators, divide up the objects suggested for cataloguing into discrete groups and treat each one as a separate 'project'. Each such project must be of a finite size and achievable within the timescale of the first phase of the overall programme. Apart from new accessions, open-ended commitments should be avoided, and every project should be complete within itself, eg a single taxonomic group of animals, the finds from a single archaeological site, or a particular collection of drawings.

Figure 7.1 Work flow diagram of typical computerized information system

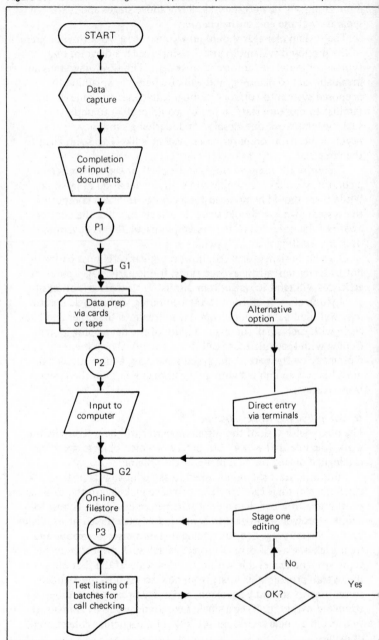

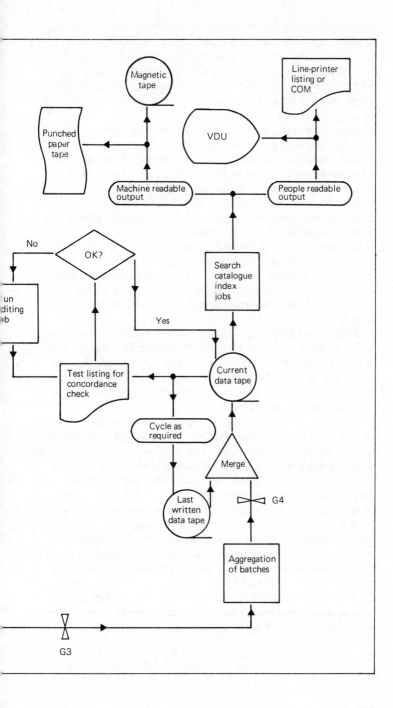

101

Ideally the assemblage of objects in a project should be such as would form a self-contained catalogue. A useful rule of thumb is to aim at projects that will produce between 1000 and 10 000 records, the optimum length varying with the discipline involved. Record length tends to be shortest in natural history and to get progressively longer through geology, archaeology/ethnology and local history, to decorative and fine art, for example.

A list of these proposed projects should be compiled, and for each the following points established:

— How big is the project? Do not trust curatorial estimates; wherever possible determine the exact number of records to be generated by having an actual count made of the objects. This usually does not take more than a few hours, and the time is well spent, because unless the target is known accurately, attempts to monitor progress will be meaningless.

— How frequently is the material accessed? The more the material is used for loans, or to answer inquiries, etc, the higher the priority it should be awarded. Scientifically important but little-known collections should not be neglected, however, as circulation of a catalogue will tend to stimulate interest in and work upon that collection.

— What is the current state of documentation? Other things being equal, a poorly catalogued collection should take precedence over one possessing a complete card catalogue, for example. For the latter, consider whether curatorial requirements might not be met more rapidly by providing a computer-generated cross index to terms in the manual catalogue.

— How good is the object data? Initially at least preference should be given to collections with the data readily available on clear labels, with a minimum of looking-up to do. This will permit rapid results to be achieved, which could politically be helpful in developing the work. Conversely, if the object data are incomplete, or a great deal of background work proves necessary to bring the information to an acceptable standard, it might be better to postpone the project pending further curation of the collection.

— What degree of curator involvement is needed? Using his knowledge of each curator's attitude towards computerization and commitment to the collection, the system manager must assess realistically the likelihood of the neccessary involvement being forthcoming. It is best to concentrate upon the converted at first, for nothing dispels the doubts of curators faster than seeing their more adventurous colleagues achieving good results.

— What resources are needed? The critical ones are the amount of staff time required, and the expected total cost of any contracted-out work such as data preparation or processing. Some examples of data capture rates found in practice are given in chapter 8, pp141.

Having compiled all this information, the system manager should then assign relative priorities to each project; these can be simply a grading into A, B or C priorities, or the whole list may be put in ranked order. The order now arrived at will need the concurrence of the curators concerned and the approval of management, which can mean that the apparent priorities become somewhat distorted by the workings of internal politics.

To retain flexibility, every primary project should be backed with a secondary one, to be worked on if the primary one is halted for any reason, or if it is completed ahead of schedule. Secondary targets are especially useful when staff are specially employed for the work on fixed-term contracts, for example with government 'job-creation' grants. Secondary targets ideally should not be monolithic, ie the results achieved will be of immediate use even if the remaining material is not catalogued for some time.

Once the work schedule has been set, the remaining stages of the operational planning may proceed.

● *Data capture*
Data capture is the process of assembling all available information about an object, and ordering it into a coherent record ready for input to the computer. The process is tedious and time consuming, and arranging for it to be done well can require a great deal of preparatory work by the system manager and curators. It is worth taking considerable trouble to get the data capture stage right, however, as it will almost certainly represent the major museum commitment in terms of manhours spent on computerization. In addition, if the data captured are not as accurate and complete as possible, an inferior information system will result. Always remember the GIGO principle: Garbage In, Garbage Out; computerization cannot of itself improve data quality.

Data standards
The primary concern of the system manager at this stage must be to establish the necessary *data standards* for the institution. This means identifying the types of information to be recorded about the objects in each project and then deciding what items of data of each type might occur. If for a given subject area a sound and detailed standard is already in use within the museum for a manual system, it will probably serve for the computerized records. Alternatively, upon investigation a widely accepted data standard, for example

103

those available from the MDAU, may be found to exist, and this should be adopted. Even if local additions such as extended thesauri are needed, the effort involved will be far less than that of setting up a satisfactory data standard from scratch. The latter is difficult and definitely to be avoided if possible, but if it must be done, follow the advice given in chapters 4 and 5.

Data input documents
The data standard having been arrived at, it now must be encapsulated within the data input document and the accompanying *coding manual*, which will give detailed rules governing the completion of each section (called a *field*) of the input document.

If MDA standards have been adopted, the MDA card can be used as a data input document, especially if the MDAU bureau service is to be used for data preparation and processing.

If it is decided the museum will design, produce and use its own input documents, and an outside data preparation service is to be used, close liaison must be maintained with the person in charge to ensure the document is acceptable to them; this precaution also applies if MDA cards are to be sent out other than to the MDAU.

Before proceeding to the detailed design of an input document, decide whether it is to be ephemeral, or to form a transaction document, or to be archival in nature; in addition is it to have general applications or be individually designed for each project?

There is no firm rule, but usually if a collection is to be computer catalogued in one stage and if it contains more than 1000 objects of one kind, such as butterflies, or shells, or china jugs or Greek pottery, etc, then a one-off input document should be considered. If the number of such objects exceeds 5000, a one-off document will almost certainly offer worthwhile savings in time and expense. For smaller or more heterogeneous collections a general document such as the MDA card for Museum Object will probably be more satisfactory.

The data input sheets used by Manchester Museum are an example of the individually designed ephemeral type. Fields are provided only for those data items relevant to a particular project (birds, shells and liverworts all have very different sheets, for example), and the sheets are destroyed once the data have been securely merged to the magnetic tape data bank and various catalogue listings have been obtained. The blank sheets are produced as computer line-printer output, using a simple program to generate the required format. This method permits the sheets to be modified easily in the light of experience as the work progresses. Although a very large number of data items can be identified as attaching to museum objects in general, any one type of object rarely requires more than 30 fields to accommodate its data.

When computerization using ephemeral input documents is being discussed, some curators express concern at the lack of a secure 'primary source document'. However, multiple copies of a magnetic data tape, especially when housed at various sites, are at least as secure a source document as, for example, a solitary bound register prone to all the accidents of fate. The MDA card is an example of the generalized document primarily intended for archival purposes. Here one card has been designed to accept the data from all types of natural history objects, for example, and the use of A5 format good card stock, with permanent ink printing means that the cards can be easily filed and stored indefinitely.

A transaction document might be one used to record loans outward which, after input to the computer, is sent with the loan; for this, coloured air-mail weight paper might prove more suitable. The systems manager should always be alert to the possibilities of sensibly using input documents in a second role, particularly if this will save staff time.

Having established the form of the input document, its layout must now be designed. This will be influenced strongly by any secondary use of the document, but it must be recognized that such influence may have a serious adverse effect upon the efficiency of the document for data preparation purposes. If the operator's eyes have to skip about the document to find data which are embedded in a mass of ruled lines or printed text, and if the tags identifying the data items are not clearly shown, input must be slowed and costs increased.

Data input documents should contain the minimum necessary amount of *structure*, ie field labels and ruled dividers; in particular explanatory notes should be as concise as possible and grouped at the end away from data fields. Labels intended to be input with the data should be printed with a type size clearly visible with average eyesight at the normal working distance of 18 − 24 inches (450 − 600 mm).

Arrange the fields in orderly rows so that the operator's eye will travel smoothly over them. Do not try to crowd too much on to the document; either use a larger format or a continuation document for excess data. Double-sided documents should be avoided, for reversing such documents slows the operator, and increases the chance that the input document order will become muddled, impeding verification (see under *data preparation*), or that data will

105

be missed. Horizontal rules defining fields should be set at multiples of one-sixth of an inch to aid typing the data; they should not be so close together as to cramp handwritten entries.

Provided it does not conflict with the above principles, the layout for the input sheet should mimic established practice. For example, the order in which the items are to be entered should be that followed naturally by a curator writing a description of the object. The system manager must obtain curatorial advice on this as every discipline tends to have its own conventions, and these should be adhered to if at all possible.

It is important to ensure that all curators comprehend that the order in which data are read into the machine has absolutely no bearing on the order in which they can be printed out, an apparently obvious point which in practice can cause initially considerable conceptual difficulty to a person with little experience of computers.

Having designed an input document, prepare a sample batch by some method such as xerography and get the curators/cataloguers to try them out; once the design is proved it may be produced in a longer run.

Completing input documents
After data capture, the most expensive stage of a computerization scheme tends to be data preparation. The cost is directly linked to the number of characters per record to be input and therefore some thought should be given at the data capture stage to reducing the number of characters entered for input to the minimum concomitant with a good quality record. The following are points to examine:
— Can structure elements be reduced? *Structure elements* here are the *field labels*, tags appended to the data items so they may be recognized by the computer program. Thus 'Hampshire' would probably mean little to most programs, but 'LOCALITY Hampshire' would enable the machine to incorporate the data into the correct part of the record. But this has required nine extra characters or *keystrokes*, remembering the space between the words is 'significant' in that it has to be typed in; if the tag was reduced to 'LOCAL' three keystrokes could be saved on *structure*. This sounds trivial, but an analysis of one year of input by Manchester Museum (some 75 000 records) showed that by removing just three keystrokes from every field label, over 90 punch operator hours could have been saved; this was equivalent to the 'free' input of a significant number of additional records, or assuming a charge of £5 per hour, a saving of £450, far from trivial for most museums.

— Can the data be abbreviated? Abbreviations may be of three
types; commonly occurring terms may be incorporated into the
institution's data-standards as *standard abbreviations*, while *local
abbreviations* are used only during one phase of one project. An
example of the latter would be to use ZL, say, to represent a
complex full citation to be repeated on a number of records in one
batch. The third type of abbreviation may be a *code;* these also
will be incorporated into the data-standard, and their use is
explained later.

Most software packages will allow for the expansion of these
abbreviations throughout a *file* of data by automatically applying
a series of standard *global edits* on input. The character combinations
used as abbreviations should be unique if possible, else the computer
may expand the text in some unexpected places!

— Can a data item be omitted altogether? If a data item will occur
on every sheet submitted for a whole project, it could be omitted
from the input sheet completely, and globally inserted to all input
for that project. Examples would be the name and code of the
institution or the name of a phylum.

Codes
Codes may be considered as dual-purpose abbreviations. A computer
program will usually sort data items only into alphabetic or numeric
order; non-alpha-numeric characters (£, *, punctuation etc) will
also have a pre-set sequence, and usually sort before the letters, with
numbers coming last, although other sequences are possible.

Unfortunately most sequences of academic terms are not
arranged alpha-numerically; for example, with the geological
succession Cambrian, Ordovician, Silurian, Devonian, Carboniferous,
Permian, . . . , Tertiary, sorting alphabetically would place the first
three terms in the correct order, but then the rest would be slotted
in to form a geologically meaningless jumble. A catalogue or index
arranged in this way would be frustrating for a geologist to use, and
certainly would not help to impress him with the utility of
computers. The problem may be overcome by writing a special
program to order the geological terms, but usually it is simpler and
more efficient to use *codes* to 'force the sort'. Thus if the code G0
replaces the term Cambrian, G1 replaces Ordovician and so on up
to G9, Tertiary, then a sort on a field GEOLCODE would correctly
order the records into the accepted geological sequence.

As a term necessarily bears a one-to-one relationship with its code
in this case, only the code need be input, with the term being added
by global edit so that both are present in the record. Other obvious

candidates for coding in this way are Egyptian dynasties, archaeological periods, and supra-generic taxa in natural history.

Codes can also aid efficient searching of data banks. Thus, providing a super-group code for 'Europe' would greatly simplify retrieving all the records of European objects; the alternative could be to search laboriously for every European country, including synonyms like 'UK' or 'GB' and terms like 'Scandinavia'. Super-group codes should form part of the data standard.

When deciding what information should be included on an input document, remember that looking up information in reference works is very time-consuming, and should be avoided on initial input wherever possible. In a direct computerization project it is usually much more efficient to input the readily available raw data to the computer, and then to use the machine to re-order and list it in ways that ensure that no item has to be looked up more than once.

For example, the material of a genus of an animal might be scattered through several drawers of an un-curated collection which is catalogued over a period of several weeks. It is quicker to obtain a listing at the end of the project giving all the records in order of genus before starting to look up the supra-generic classification, rather than doing it every time a specimen of that genus is met with during cataloguing. One global edit then puts the necessary information into all relevant records.

The advantage of this approach is fourfold
— non-specialist cataloguers can input and check the raw data rapidly, and look up can be done at leisure by the curator who, knowing the subject, will be more efficient at it.
— it is easier consistently to record the validation authority for all added information.
— the danger of having multiple spellings of complex names such as *'Streptaxacea Haplotrematidae'* entered inadvertently is effectively removed when such names have to be entered only once. The machine edit will be error-free, so if that one entry is correct the rest need not be checked.
— the number of data characters to be written and to be data prepared is reduced.

Standards manual
A complete data standard for a museum will form a substantial reference work, and a copy should be available to everyone concerned with the computerization scheme. It is a good idea, however, to provide cataloguers with a summary of the standards relevant to their particular project; this will save time searching for relevant information in the full manual and, much more important, will increase the probability of the standards being adhered to

during data capture. If possible, the essentials should be reduced to a single sheet of paper so that the cataloguer can see everything at a glance. Such a 'mini-manual' can carry short lists of codes or preferred terms, but in some disciplines it will have to be supplemented with a thesaurus. The instructions should be kept as simple and unambiguous as possible, and free text should be allowed in as many fields as possible. Controlled vocabularies slow down the work and should be restricted to those fields from which it is intended to generate an index, or that will be searched frequently.

Starting to catalogue
Before actually starting to catalogue, the staff concerned will need to work out the *modus operandi*. A work-site must be chosen and at it assembled the data standard manual, input documents, any special implements or materials, such as entomological forceps or cotton wool, and any other reference works needed, such as an atlas, gazetteer, field notebooks, etc. If possible objects to be catalogued should also be brought adjacent to the work-site, and suitable temporary storage provided. Sometimes for conservation or other reasons the objects have to be catalogued in a store-room or gallery; in that case a suitable trolley should be provided to carry the work-site to the objects. Time spent on simple work study at this stage is rarely wasted, and could well lead to a considerable increase in throughput of records. The cataloguers themselves should be encouraged to suggest more convenient ways of doing things.

As the objects are catalogued they should be stored, temporarily at least, in an order that will facilitate re-finding at the data checking stage; registered number order is often convenient. Each object should be marked or tagged as it is catalogued to prevent future confusion about which objects have been dealt with. A simple program could be used to generate and print-out sequences of registered numbers to be cut up and stored with the objects; this would help also to prevent accidental duplication of registered numbers when more than one cataloguer is working on a given collection. An alternative or additional method would be to marry a computer produced label with the object at the data-checking stage.

● *Data preparation and input*
Before the data assembled on to the input document can be fed into the computer they must be converted into machine-readable form. This can be done either by the cataloguers performing direct-entry, or *via* a data preparation operator.

True *direct-entry* by-passes the input document completely; the cataloguer sits at the keyboard of a computer terminal and types in the information as it comes to hand. This method can be rather inefficient unless the cataloguer is also a competent typist, and it assumes that enough terminals will be provided to permit simultaneous input by several people as well as providing terminal time for on-line editing and retrieval. However, the provision of an interactive program to prompt the cataloguers, and to provide them with controlled vocabulary lists as needed, can remove the need for a *coding manual* and thesauri while permitting high-quality input.

A direct-entry approach in a big scheme will mean considerable capital outlay, and multiple terminals require either multiple lines to the computer or the use of an additional device to permit the inputs from several terminals to be sent down a single line.

Data input documents and pencils are very much cheaper than terminals of any kind, and for most museums the data input document followed by data preparation will be the most suitable course to follow.

Data preparation may be treated as a step completely separate from data capture and from data processing. After data capture it is the most expensive part of the whole operation and every effort should be made to utilize local resources, exploring the avenues suggested earlier under *hardware* (p91). If these all prove fruitless the museum will either have to provide the machinery and people itself, or it will have to use the services of a data prep bureau.

If the work is to be contracted out, where MDA cards are in use the MDAU should be approached first, for they are experienced in working with these somewhat complex documents. Otherwise a commercial concern can be used; their charges will, however, be at a commercial level, although by accepting a slow turnaround it may be possible to negotiate a cheaper rate.

There are various methods of making the data *machine-readable*. The oldest is the use of a punched card, such as the 80 column Hollerith card, but these are expensive and bulky, and card punches are expensive to buy and maintain. Punched paper tapes may be used; the 8-hole version should be used as the 7-hole type is now essentially obsolete. Reading large volumes of data into the machine *via* paper tape can be a slow and error-prone operation, but as the method is obsolescent commercially, sometimes redundant tape punches can be acquired free from a more affluent organization and used for data prep within the museum. However, maintenance of these old machines can be difficult, and new paper tape punches, possibly as an add-on accessory to an existing terminal, could prove more satisfactory.

The use of *OCR*, optical character recognition, and *MCR*, magnetic-ink character recognition, by museums is unlikely to be feasible, since expensive specialized equipment is needed both to produce the input document and to read the data into the machine. A related method, mark-sensing input, is too restricted in scope to offer much assistance to museums.

Currently the most efficient way to input data is *via* some form of magnetized medium; this can be in the form of a disc (rigid or flexible, the latter called a 'floppy'), or as a tape held in a cassette, in a cartridge or on a reel. At present the most favoured medium is the floppy disc, which is a circular piece of thin plastic rather like the flexible 'demonstration record' sometimes used in commercial postal promotions.

As explained above under *hardware*, floppies can be used to enhance the storage capacity of a microcomputer. If a small computer is linked to a *mainframe* it can be used as an *intelligent terminal*, permitting a batch of data to be typed in, stored on a floppy disc, checked and edited before being sent down the link to the mainframe for later processing. Equally, a subset of records from the mainframe *data bank* can be selectively retrieved over the link and stored on a floppy disc for local interrogation or manipulation.

Bureaux can usually produce the data in any of the forms mentioned above, but for preference either floppy disc or magnetic tape should be chosen. Before commencing a major project it is essential to conduct compatibility trials to make sure that the data from the bureau can be read by the computer you are using.

The charges of commercial bureaux are normally stated in terms of 'per thousand keystrokes'; as a guide, rates being quoted in the UK in mid-1980 ranged from 45p to 90p/1000 keystrokes, depending on the complexity of the input document. Keystrokes are quoted rather than characters because all blanks between words and all punctuation have to be typed in by depressing keys, and have to be charged for.

When data are prepared by a bureau they can be verified also. This means one operator types in the data and then a second operator re-types the same data on a verifier, a machine that reads the card or disc produced by the first operator and compares the contents with what is being typed by the second operator; any discrepancy causes an error to be indicated, and the operator then takes the appropriate action.

Input
The term *input* is used as a verb to describe the act of reading data into the machine, eg 'the data were input', and as a noun for the file of data itself, eg 'three batches of input'; *output* is used in the same ways.

The prepared data will usually be input by the operators at the computer site because:
— this is obviously sensible if it has been prepared there,
— transmitting bulky data over a link-line is expensive and slow, so if the preparation is done at the museum or by an independent bureau it will be more efficient physically to transport the cards or tapes to the site for input.

Whether bureau-prepared data come first to the museum or are forwarded direct to the computer site for input will depend on local circumstances, but the method chosen will have implications for the monitoring of the workflow (see p122).

Wherever possible it should be arranged that all relevant *global edits* to expand abbreviations and insert standard information are done automatically by the machine on every batch of information at input time.

● *Data processing*
When the data have been input, processing may commence; the exact method of working will depend on the *file-handling* facilities available on the computer installation and upon the software package in use. The method outlined in this section is based on that used by Manchester Museum, but all information processing schemes must follow a broadly similar path. The information goes through a cycle of test-listing and editing, followed by *merging* into a *data bank* from which, after second-stage *concordance editing*, catalogues and indexes may be produced and upon which selective retrieval searches may be done.

It is recommended that the input data should be divided into batches of records such that each batch, called a *file* on the computer, contains approximately 10000 to 12000 characters (ie 15—50 records depending on the subject). At Manchester Museum this has been found to be the optimum length for first-stage files, short enough to prevent fatigue during checking, but not so short that the number of files formed causes monitoring problems.

First-stage test-listing cycle
As soon as any global edits have been completed, a listing of the newly input file should be produced for checking, if possible with each line numbered automatically by the machine to assist editing. This listing is checked against the original sources, ideally by *call checking*, when one person reads the listing while another calls out the relevant data. Basic errors, such as overlooked, mis-spelt, incorrectly transcribed or mis-punched data are noted on the listing

as in correcting a galley proof. Errors must be circled or underlined, *never* obliterated, for whoever edits the file will need some means of identifying the old text which is to be changed.

Someone sitting at a terminal can then, using the 'marked up' listing, edit the file using the machine *text editor;* nowadays sophisticated text editors are available on all large machines. Once edited, the file is re-listed and again checked. If more errors are found the cycle is repeated, but if none is found the data are pronounced 'clean' and may be passed to the next stage of processing.

Forming a data bank

As the batches of clean data accumulate, it is necessary to assemble them into an information file or *data bank,* upon which the processing package can work. The bulk of a museum's data will be stored on magnetic tapes, at least until *on-line mass storage* becomes very much cheaper, and it is these tapes that will form the data bank. A 'standard' computer tape is 0.5 inch wide and 2400 feet long (12.7 mm x 732 m); the amount of information it will hold mainly depends upon the *packing density* used. At 800 *bits per inch (bpi)* a 2400 foot tape will hold in the order of 6×10^6 characters; other packing densities commonly found are 1600 *bpi* and 6250 *bpi.*

Until now the data have been in 'text' form, but all processing packages store the information in their own unique *internal format.* Therefore to form a data bank records have to be manipulated by that part of the package that forms these internal records; for example, a FAMULUS 'original EDIT' or a GOS 'BUILD'. During this conversion it is possible sometimes to reorganize and add to records; GOS is particularly powerful in the way data can be manipulated during the BUILD process. Once the initial data bank has been formed, new records are usually added to it by a process of *merging;* normally the data bank will be stored sorted according to the contents of certain key fields, and so a MERGE program will sort the new records into the same order and then run through the data bank slotting them into their correct positions. This method is much more efficient, ie uses less machine time, than appending the new records to the file and then doing a massive re-sort of the whole file. The only time merging is not necessary is when the data are filed in an arbitrary serial order, such as by new accession number, so that new records need only be added to the end of the file.

Before merging it is better to append together several batches from stage one to form a longer 'aggregate' file, allowing more efficient processing and reducing the cost per record of any fixed overheads incurred in running a MERGE job. An aggregate file composed of about ten batches has been found convenient at Manchester.

Second-stage editing cycle: concordance checking
Although the data are now free of basic errors, it will be found that variant terms have crept in, no matter how tightly terminology was controlled at the data capture stage. To remove such variations the data will have to be concorded. Consider, for example, the following:
Smith A   Smith, A   Smith,A   Smith, A.
Although in a given file these all may be known to refer to the same person, they could appear as four separate entries in a computer-produced name index, and each would have to be specified for a successful selective retrieval search; thus at least three of these names would need editing to bring them into concordance with the agreed format for names in the museum data standards.

To examine the concordance of terms in a data bank, test indexes should be produced periodically, the interval between such indexes depending upon the rate new records are added to the data bank. How many new records merged justify a fresh index is for the system manager to judge, but the cost of processing and the desires of the relevant curator(s) will be important factors affecting this decision.

These test indexes should be used also by curators for the insertion of extra information from reference books as suggested in the section on *data capture* (p108); the indexes will also highlight any inconsistent spellings in need of correction.

Test catalogues should also be produced soon after a new data bank is formed, so that the need for any explanatory tags can be seen. For example, the significance of a collector's name may not be clear from its context within a printed-out record, but the insertion of the tag 'collected by;' in front of all such names would solve this problem.

Test catalogues and indexes can be used immediately by curators working with the collections, without waiting for the fully corrected version; indeed, intensive use by curatorial staff and visitors should be encouraged so that the maximum number or errors can be found and corrected in the shortest possible time. A standardized routine for reporting errors is essential.

Adding to or correcting records, or deleting redundant records will be done using the EDITOR section of the processing package; some packages have more sophisticated editors than others.

If the records in a data bank are kept sorted in the same order as that most often used in producing catalogues, appreciable amounts of processing time can be saved. However, if the records are wanted frequently in more than one order, it might be worth maintaining two or more data banks each in a different order. Although this will save processing time at the cataloguing stage, some of the advantage is lost as now there are several data banks to be kept up to date. Therefore the question of more sophisticated data-storage techniques is one the system manager will have to examine very carefully. (Crennell & Marsh, 1979).

Data security

Computerized data banks are expensive to generate, so it is important to guard them against loss or corruption. If a time-sharing mainframe is being used, the operating system should provide a periodic *dumping* facility to guard against data loss from the *filestore*. This means that all data entered or changed since the last *dump* are automatically copied out on to magnetic tapes. Then if because of a power failure, for example, all the filestore data are lost, everything present up to the last *dump* will be regenerated by a *system restore* procedure when the machine is restarted. Dumps usually take place at 6, 12 or 24 hourly intervals depending on the installation. Thus all data going through the initial editing cycle are protected until they are merged to the data bank. Magnetic tapes are *not* secured by the system dump, however, and they are *insecure* storage media because they can become unreadable for several reasons, such as wear, various forms of operator error, or from no apparent cause! A magnetic tape fail is usually total and no recovery is possible. Thus prudence dictates keeping a minimum of three copies of every data tape.

These copies should be cycled on the 'grandfather-father-son' principle, illustrated in Figure 7.2. If the three tapes are called T1, T2 and T3, then the first batch of data, A, will be *written* to (ie recorded upon) T1. To add batch B, T1 is remounted on the machine, the data *read* (ie copied) into the filestore, a processing *job* run to merge the new data, and the file A+B written to T2. When batch C is to be added the operation is repeated, only this time T2 is *read* and T3 is *written* At this juncture T1 (grandfather) contains batch A only, T2 (father) contains A+B and T3 (son) contains A+B+C. For batch D, T 3 is read, T1 is written, and the whole cycle starts again. The tapes will have to be cycled also when editing the data bank; merging and editing are known collectively as *updating*. *Read only* jobs, to produce a catalogue/index or to run a search, need only to mount the 'son' tape and no tape cycling is required.

If when the 'son' is mounted it fails (ie cannot be read by the machine), the 'father' must be called for, but the last merged batch of data will have been lost from the data bank. It is therefore important to retain a batch of data on the filestore until that

115

Figure 7.2 Showing cycling of data-tapes

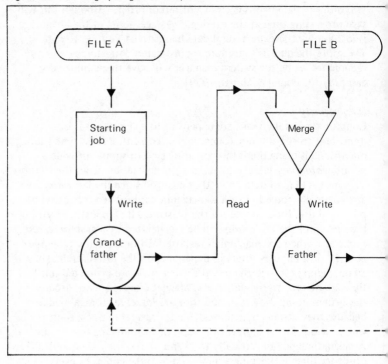

particular batch has been *secured* on all three generations of tapes. If both son and father fail, recourse must be made to the grandfather, and the last two batches will need remerging to the data bank.

Given reasonable operating arrangements, a tape fail certainly should not occur more than once in every hundred tape mounts. Thus the probability of all three generations of a data bank failing simultaneously is at least a million to one against. If a triple fail *should* happen, the data bank could be regenerated if the 'backup' precautions outlined below have been taken. Any tape that has not been accessed for six months should be cleaned and rewound by the operators; if this procedure is not automatic at the computer site, the system manager will be responsible for ensuring that it is done. For complete safety, all tapes should be read at least once a year and, ideally, should be rewritten at the same time.

116

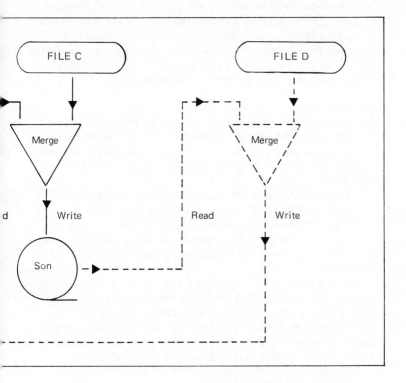

Security backup

The three generations of tapes discussed above need to be stored near the computer so that they can be mounted as required by the operators. However, the accidental or deliberate destruction of the installation is a credible event, and such destruction could result in the loss of a data bank representing many man years of work by a museum, even though any printed-out catalogues, etc, would still exist. It is strongly recommended therefore that additional copies of all data tapes are kept at another site against such an eventuality. Copies of all *file handling routines* and any other programs should be stored in this way as well.

If the computer tape library is destroyed, there is a high probability the processing unit also will be out of action. This could be an embarassing situation if the museum has come to rely upon the computer files for smooth daily running. It is therefore advisable to make contingency arrangements with another computer site to run your processing until the 'home' site is operational again. Such arrangements should be put to a practical test, as even computer sites apparently operating identical machinery in the same way can possess subtle differences; such compatibility tests should be repeated at six to twelve month intervals because no system remains static. The time to find out your tapes will not read at the backup site is before, not after, the home site is destroyed!

Confidentiality

It is not possible to guarantee confidentiality of information stored in a computer. The only certain way to maintain confidentiality is not to put the information into the machine; what could be input is a cross-reference to a manual file held securely by the museum authorities.

Some processing packages permit *encryption* of information, ie the garbling of information so that it can be made intelligible only by the use of a key. This technique should be used sparingly, for there are clever people in the computer world to whom the discovery of *cryptic data* is an instant challenge, and *any* code can be broken eventually.

Another approach, if the data are voluminous, is to store them on a tape or disc which is then physically removed from the computer site and stored securely within the museum, being returned only when the data have to be read. Even this method is not totally secure, however, for it would be a trivial job for an operator to make a copy of the data during its brief visit to the installation.

The use of *system traps* or *passwords* affords only a very low level of confidentiality, for all such devices perforce must be transparent to the installation operators; the utility of such devices is to guard against the accidental overwriting or erasure of tapes and files.

Publication and searching

Whether to issue the accumulated data in some published form (see *Output*, below) is necessarily a policy decision for the institution concerned, but if it is done it must be decided also how to treat subsequent updates. Certainly all changes to a data bank after it has been published should be tagged in some way; such updates could be issued periodically as supplements to the original catalogue, or a complete new edition could be produced at longer intervals.

In addition, or as an alternative, to formal publication, the question of *on-line* access to the data bank should be considered. As more and more museums computerize, they will become equipped to dial-up data banks elsewhere (eg the British Museum *Art and Archaeology data bank*). Whether a given data bank is made available in this way obviously depends upon technical considerations, but is also a policy decision for management. If access is provided, is it to be free or charged, public or restricted to registered users? The same questions have to be answered if it is decided instead to offer a 'search on demand' service, replying to telephoned or written inquiries with computer listings of records selectively retrieved from the data banks.

● *Output*
To be of use, the results of data processing need to be *output* in some way. Although a *machine-readable* version of the data, for storage or transfer to another processing system, is also termed *output,* most output will be in plain text, 'people-readable' form. Generally the records output are in an order different to that in which they were input and/or the arrangement of information within the record may be altered; sometimes selected items of information are suppressed on output, although such items remain recorded on the data bank.

The data may be output in several different ways, although few installations will offer all the options; the method chosen will depend upon the intended use of the output.

Display upon the television screen of a VDU, or *Visual Display Unit,* may be preferred for listing small parts of a *file* to assist on-line update or correction editing, or for examining the results of a selective retrieval search.

A printed listing on paper is more useful for marking-up correction edits, and for the production of catalogues and indexes for use within the museum.

Printing output within the museum
There are two main types of printer that could be sited within the museum:
— teletype terminals. The print facilities on these are intended for recording input text and commands, and for printing out short messages from the computer. They are too slow for it to be practical to list long files upon them; their usual printing rates are 10 or 30 characters per second, although speeds up to 120 characters a second can be obtained on sophisticated terminals.
— portable printers. These are faster than terminals, with printing rates up to 250 lines per minute (*lpm*), but they may not prove durable if heavily used (see page 91).

Both sorts of device may use pre-formed typefaces, operating by a variety of mechanisms. One that seems to be gaining popularity for small printers has a print head with each typeface on a separate stalk radiating from a central control arm, with the typefaces selected by rotating the print head; from their resemblance to the flower they are called *daisy-wheel* printers.

Also popular now are *matrix printers;* in these the characters are formed from nine short lines printed by 'pins' arranged in a matrix similar to that used by pocket calculators to display digits. Matrix printers are quieter, more reliable and capable of higher print speeds than terminals using conventional typing technology. Other terminals and printers on the market use heat sensitive or electro-sensitive paper; they are fast and quiet, but the special paper can prove costly.

The limit on printing speed within the museum may be dictated not by the device used but by the transmission speed of the line linking the printer to the mainframe. If only one link is available, while it is being used to transmit long files it could be unavailable for use with other terminal devices, and if a telephone line is used then the call charges could become sizable if many long files are transmitted.

Printing at the mainframe site
For the reasons indicated above, most museums will find it best when outputting lengthy files to use the *high-speed impact line-printers* available at all mainframe sites, and to limit any local printer to listing files of 1000 lines or under; this limit should prove adequate for most output required urgently within the museum. *High-speed* means printing rates up to 2000 *lpm, impact* means printing by striking type against plain paper with a ribbon between, and *line* means that effectively an entire line of type is printed at once.

There are two types of line-printer, *chain* and *drum.* The former, where the individual typefaces are carried on a continuous horizontally rotating band, normally give a better looking result than the drum printers, where the separate vertically rotating typeface drums can easily get out of register and produce wavy lines of type.

Printer listings are invaluable for reference and annotation within the museum, and although several copies of a given catalogue may be output for distribution for criticism by curators elsewhere, such listings are slow in production. Printer listings are also bulky, expensive to send through the mail, and awkward to use, and it is quite impractical to consider the wide dissemination of museum catalogues in this form.

Microform output

Increasingly, computer sites are installing a COM, or Computer Output on Microform, peripheral device as an alternative to line-printing long files. The standard output formats from these are 16 mm microfilm and/or a 3 x 5 inch (76 mm x 127 mm) microfiche at x24 reduction, giving 72 frames per fiche, or x48 reduction, giving 270 frames per fiche.

Microfiche, simple and cheap to produce, cheaply and easily duplicated and mailed, offer museums an excellent way of distributing catalogues to other institutions. The economic outlook indicates that more and more academic publishing will be available in microfiche, not just computer produced data, and the acquisition of a good quality microfiche reader should be a priority for all museums not yet so equipped.

If the computer in use does not provide COM, the data can be read out on to a magnetic tape from which specialist bureaux can prepare and duplicate the microfiche.

Printing computer produced catalogues

A compromise approach could be to print just the introduction and indexes to a catalogue, and to bind these with the microfiche 'pocketed' within the cover. This not only makes using the fiche much easier and helps to prevent it getting mislaid by the recipient, but also permits the publication to carry the house-style of the originating museum.

The generally poor quality of impact line-printer output makes it unsuitable for use as a master for reprographic devices such as Xerox or Multilith machines. Considerable success has been achieved at Manchester Museum in making such masters by punching out the prepared catalogue as a paper tape, then feeding this through a tape-operated electric typewriter. Using a reprographic quality carbon ribbon, the data are typed on to A3 sheets which are then reduced to A4 masters. If, as here, the equipment is already available, the process is cheap but slow, taking five to ten minutes per page to type.

A faster and simpler method would be to print out the finished catalogue on to a magnetic tape or disc, suitable for use by a commercial computer-typesetting bureau.

The peripatetic collection

The idea of the 'peripatetic curator' has been much discussed in museum circles in the last decade; by speeding up and simplifying the process of producing and distributing collection information, computerization will, it is to be hoped, assist the emergence of the 'peripatetic collection'.

By making distant experts aware of the content of its collections, especially by providing full details of the raw data attached to them, museums will encourage those experts to comment constructively on the data and to work on the material, by means of loans or visits, so helping the further curation of the collections.

The inquiry snowball

As the ability of the museum staff to conduct searches of the computer data bank becomes known, scholarly inquiries may be expected to increase dramatically in number. The growth of this 'inquiry snowball' will be hastened as curators come to realize that many questions it was not sensible previously to ask can now be answered simply and quickly by interrogation of a computerized data bank.

For example, although a museum with complete, fully cross-indexed card catalogues could trace all the material it held from a given locality, it certainly could not find and transcribe these records with the use of only two minutes of staff time; in most instances, the large amount of staff time needed would preclude the answering of that inquiry. But two minutes is all it should take to type a search inquiry into the computer, which would then retrieve *and print-out* the required records; such a listing could be cheaper than the cost of photocopying numerous cards, and a lot less troublesome, while it is certainly less error-prone than manual transcription of records.

● Monitoring the system

It is important that adequate monitoring is built into the system from the start. The passage of batches towards the data banks should be noted at several control points or 'gates'; typical positions for control 'gates' are shown in Figure 7.1 as G1 — G4. Keeping note of the records forming a given batch would normally be done by the cataloguer or the curator responsible, but the allocation of unique titles or *filenames* to the batches would be controlled by the system manager.

As well as gates, 'pounds' are needed to smooth the workflow, and to permit different priorities to be assigned to the processing of different types of information. 'Pounds' are places where data can be allowed to accumulate should there be a hold-up in the system; their positions are marked P1 — P3 in Figure 7.1. P1 will contain any backlog of completed data input sheets, P2 punchcards or tapes, and P3 the data being edited on the computer filestore. The capacity of P3 generally will be limited, and P2 is unavailable either if direct input is used or if the data are prepared elsewhere and input without returning to the museum. If P2 is unavailable, very tight control will be needed at G2 to prevent the system becoming clogged.

The cycling of data tapes (see Figure 7.2) should be done automatically, although the exact method used will vary from machine to machine. Details of tape updates should be logged automatically, as should all tape failures and their causes, for this will permit unreliable tapes, or tape-decks, to be pinpointed and changed.

Terminal occupation, ie the time spent using an on-line terminal, should be logged; statistics for each user and for each project should be kept. Machine processing time also should be logged for each project. The system manager will need a regular printout showing details of the files actually on the machine filestore, so that those that are finished with can be erased or purged; controlling filestore usage is usually one of the more intractable problems faced by the system manager.

Computers generally produce a wealth of logs, statistics and records of work done, and a degree of caution is required in selecting what to extract and keep; it is all too easy to become swamped with computer output. Try to determine exactly which items of information it is helpful to have available, and for how long. Often it will prove adequate merely to keep the last listing, or those for the past month, or else to retain just summaries of the information.

All the monitoring information gathered should be carefully filed, for from it the system manager will need to produce various statistical summaries. The exact nature of these summaries will differ depending whether they are intended for use by senior management, for discussing future resources allocations with the computer managers, or for checking on the work efficiency of cataloguers. The figures will be invaluable in planning future phases of the project work.

Quality control

As mentioned earlier, the quality of information that can be retrieved from a data bank can be no higher than the quality of the information fed in. The machine can do no more than sort and select records to assist the curators in enhancing the data, but the actual enhancements have to come from the human brain.

Maintenance of academic standards in recording is the responsibility of the originating curator, moderated in the usual fashion by the criticism of his or her peers. To assist this latter process it is useful to circulate pre-production line-printer listing or 'galleys' to a few selected fellow experts, before formally publishing a catalogue.

Maintenance of data standards within a record is ultimately the responsibility of the system manager. This includes watching over the use of any controlled vocabulary, and checking that each record has all its essential data entered and that, as far as can be determined, no logical inconsistencies exist in the data. In addition, checks must be done to ensure that the data are correctly formated for manipulating with the chosen package. As many of these checks as possible should be done by the machine; several packages include routines that check for basic errors on input.

Much of the system manager's time will be occupied in keeping track of documents, decks of punchcards, magnetic tape, files of data on the computer, and output; the control of all these elements must be tightly organized if chaos is to be prevented. When a team of people is involved, the responsibilities of each member must be precisely defined, to ensure no tasks fail to be done because everyone thought someone else would do it; equally disastrous can be two people each doing a single task — both editing the same file, for example, which could garble or even destroy the data.

Finally all the people involved in the computerization scheme should meet regularly and frequently to discuss progress, and to agree priorities and modifications. With large schemes it is useful also to hold smaller meetings at longer intervals to examine in detail each individual project.

Reviewing the system
Once the computerization system is running smoothly, the system manager should continue to scrutinize every task to determine whether, in the light of experience, it can be streamlined or even abolished. All computer facilities are dynamic, with new versions of operating systems, compilers, and other software constantly being implemented; the system manager must be alert to all these changes so as to prevent any degradation of the museum system and to make sure full advantage is taken of any useful new facilities.

● Summary

Computerization needs more resources for putting information into
the system than do the equivalent manual methods, but yields
considerable savings in
— keeping records up-to-date
— producing post-coordinate indexes
— retrieving and transcribing information from the system
— disseminating collection information

Management must define clearly the museum-oriented objectives of
the system; the machines (*hardware*) and the programs (*software*) to
be used need to be chosen with care, and definite allocations of
money and staff-time must be made.

To obtain satisfactory results without incurring needless costs, a
system approach must be used. Each stage of the work should be
planned in detail. The whole operation should be a team effort,
and a museum-trained person should be in charge.

Capturing the data is the most expensive part of the work, and the
system must be designed to make this aspect as efficient as possible;
it is this stage that is likely to govern the true overall cost of this
system.

Preparing the data for input to the computer is also expensive, and
all the available options should be examined carefully, to obtain
the maximum saving.

To obtain the best results, the machine-processing and output stages
must be well organized, but in terms of time and money these are
very much the cheapest part of the system. To see the true economic
picture, the cost of computing work must be weighed against the
staff-time it saves and the greater power of the overall system.

Once running, the system should be monitored closely to ensure that
all is going to plan, and ways should be sought of streamlining and
enhancing the system.

● Short glossary of computer jargon

batch-mode, *see* p 93
bug, an error in a *program*
call-checking, *see* p 112
central processing unit, the part of the electronic *hardware* where
    data is actually manipulated by the machine during processing
codes, *see* p107
coding manual, *see* p104
COM, computer output on microform, *see* p121
compiler, *see high-level language*
concordance editing, *see* p112
CPU, *see central processing unit*
daisywheel printer, *see* p120
data bank, *see* p104
— base, *see* p104
— element, one discrete item of data to be manipulated by the
    processing package
— standards, *see* p103
de-bugging, correcting errors in *programs*
direct entry, *see* p104
dump, dumping, copying out information from the *filestore* for
    security purposes; dumping does not delete the data from
    the filestore
encryption, *see* p118
field, area delimited on *input document* to contain one set of
    data items
file, a set of records held in the computer *memory* or *filestore*
— handling routines, *programs* to organize *files* before and after
    processing
— store, *random access memory* where *files* can be held *on-line*
floppy disc, *see* p91
global edit, the execution of a given edit, or change, throughout a
    file automatically by the machine
hardware, *see* p88
highlevel language, a method of writing instructions to the computer
    that is oriented towards the user application rather than to the
    machine; the language is converted to machine instructions by a
    compiler, or conversion *program*
implementation, the process of getting a new piece of *software* to
    work, or 'run', on a computer
input, *see* p111
interactive, *see* p 93

internal format, the way in which a *processing package* represents
data for storage; each package has its own internal format which, if
printed out, would appear as gibberish to humans

K, abbreviation for 'thousand', but in computing terms it actually
equals 1024 characters, eg '48k of store' means a storage
capacity of 49,152 characters

liveware, *see* p88

line printer, *see* p 120

machine-readable, data in a form, such as punched cards or magnetic
tape, that can be 'read' by a computer

main-frame, a large computer, usually *timesharing* in that several
operations, or jobs, can be run at the same time; generally
associated with a range of *peripheral* equipment

mass storage, large scale, quick-access memory connected *on-line*
to the computer

matrix printer, *see* p 120

MCR, *see* p110

merging, *see* p112

Modem, short for Modulator/demodulator, GPO term for a device
enabling a *terminal*, or other equipment, to be connected to a
computer *via* a telephone line

mount, act of placing a magnetic tape on to a tape-deck so that
it may be used by the computer

OCR, *see* p110

on-line, connected directly to the *central processing unit*

operating system, *see* p98

optical character recognition, *see* p110

output, *see* p111

passwords, a method of restricting access to an *on-line file* or to a
tape; not secure as passwords must be transparent to the
system operators

peripheral, devices around the main computer but connected to it;
generally used for *input* and *output*, eg line-printers,
terminals, tapedecks

processor, *see central processing unit*

processing package, *see* p94

program, a set of instructions to cause a computer to perform a
given function; by convention always spelt as shown

software, *see* p88

— package, *see* p98

source listing, see p94

structure, *see* p 105

system editor, a *program* permitting text to be altered, added to or
 deleted on the *filestore,* usually provided by the computer
 manufacturer, and operated by simple commands such as
 REPLACE, DELETE, INSERT etc
traps, indicators or 'flags' attached to *files* that may be set 'on' or
 'off' by the user, to guard against accidental corruption of a
 file on the *filestore.* For example, a file may be trapped against
 erasure; any subsequent attempt to erase that *file* will then fail
 until the user opens the traps again
terminal, strictly any input or output device, but now generally
 reserved for a keyboarded station connected to the computer
text editor, *see system editor*
updating, *see* p 115
user interface, the parts of a computer scheme seen by a user, eg a
 curator; consists of such things as the input documents and any
 commands for use at *on-line terminals*
VDU, visual display unit, a *terminal* that uses a television screen to
 display any text being sent to or from the computer

● References

Crennell, K M and Marsh, E 'Computerisation of the Rutherford
Laboratory catalogue' *Program* 13 (2) April 1979, 73–84

Gautier, T G 'The changing nature of entomological collections –
4 Electronic data processing in systematic collections' *Entomologia
Scandinavia* 9 September 1978, 161–168

Hancock, E G and Pettitt, C W 'A register of collections and collectors
in North West England (Bottany, Geology and Zoology):The first
edition, March 1979' *Museums journal* 79(4) March 1980, 185–7

McAllister D E 'The compleat minicomputer cataloguing and
research system for a museum' *Curator* 21(1) 1978, 63–91

Mumford, E and Henshall, D *A participative approach to computer
systems design* Associated Business Publications, 1978

Museum Documentation Association
Museum Documentation Advisory Unit
Imperial War Museum
Duxford Airfield
Duxford
Cambridgeshire CB2 4QR

Chapter 8
Using human resources in information handling

Information-handling systems are created by people, operated by people, and dedicated to the purpose of serving people. Some systems make it difficult to maintain faith in this proposition, but it is nevertheless a true one. It follows that, at all the stages of analysis, definition of requirements, through planning to implementation and monitoring, the interests of two groups of people should take first place. These groups are:
— those whose work contributes in any way to the creation and handling of information resources
— those who use the information resources.

The two groups of course overlap to a certain extent, and the core of people who both generate or handle and use the products are a key group. They should therefore be actively involved at all stages of the process. If they are, and if they are helped to acquire knowledge of concepts and methods of information handling which are unfamiliar to them, they will be able to contribute to implementation and development of the system from their own specialized knowledge and skills. The system will thus have a much better chance of meeting real needs and working successfully than it would if it were either introduced over the heads of those most affected, or left to be run by specialists.

This chapter is devoted to the consideration of ways in which the people concerned with information handling can use their time and skills to the best advantage in making the system work for their benefit. Figure 8.1, which sets out the sequence of activities that should be involved in planning and implementing a system of information handling, will be used as a framework. Many aspects of the process have already been discussed in earlier chapters, but there they were treated from the point of view of their actual content — what questions need to be asked in order to define information needs, for instance. In this chapter, they will be looked at from the point of view of the people concerned in the activities, and the emphasis will be on how people can successfully work together to achieve ends which they themselves have agreed on. This is an aspect too often neglected, perhaps because the attitudes and feelings of people towards changes in ways of working are thought of as being

Figure 8.1 The use of human resources in the development of information systems

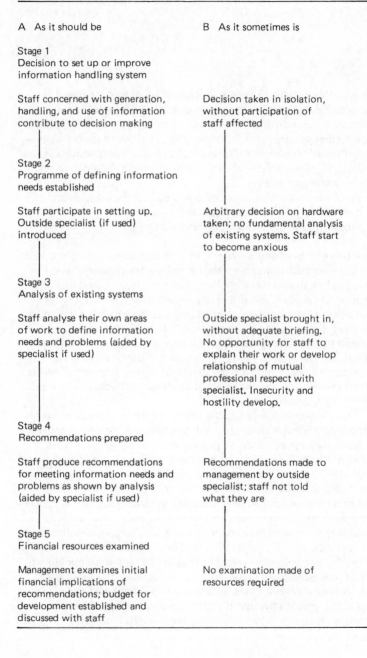

A As it should be	B As it sometimes is
Stage 1 Decision to set up or improve information handling system	
Staff concerned with generation, handling, and use of information contribute to decision making	Decision taken in isolation, without participation of staff affected
Stage 2 Programme of defining information needs established	
Staff participate in setting up. Outside specialist (if used) introduced	Arbitrary decision on hardware taken; no fundamental analysis of existing systems. Staff start to become anxious
Stage 3 Analysis of existing systems	
Staff analyse their own areas of work to define information needs and problems (aided by specialist if used)	Outside specialist brought in, without adequate briefing. No opportunity for staff to explain their work or develop relationship of mutual professional respect with specialist. Insecurity and hostility develop.
Stage 4 Recommendations prepared	
Staff produce recommendations for meeting information needs and problems as shown by analysis (aided by specialist if used)	Recommendations made to management by outside specialist; staff not told what they are
Stage 5 Financial resources examined	
Management examines initial financial implications of recommendations; budget for development established and discussed with staff	No examination made of resources required

Figure 8.1 continued

A   As it should be   B   As it sometimes is

Stage 6
Overall system
configuration agreed

Management and staff agree on   Management makes commitment
overall pattern for system   to system designed by
which can be implemented within   outside specialist, without
budget available (aided by   consulting staff
specialist if used)

Stage 7
Detailed planning

Staff (aided by specialist if   Details of system worked out
used) decide on mehtods, hardware   without staff participation
and software;
system documentation drafted
and tested;
routines and procedures
established & documented;
monitoring procedures set up

Stage 8
Implementation programme agreed

Phased programme of implementation   No implementation
jointly decided on   programme developed

Stage 9
Training for implementation

Training given to key   No training programme. Staff
staff who will implement   told they are to start
                                       operating new system from a
                                       given date

Figure 8.1 continued

A   As it should be   B   As it sometimes is

Stage 10
Implementation — pilot phase

Phased implementation starts.   Insecurity and resentment
Staff monitor progress (aided   mount. Some staff carry out
by specialist, if used), make   instructions without under-
necessary changes.   standing or commitment; others
Development proposals put   withdraw from situation and
forward by staff, agreed,   refuse to have any part of it.
implemented and monitored   Old system discontinued before
                                       new one fully tested. New
                                       system runs into difficulties.
                                       No monitoring, hence no
                                       possibility of learning from
                                       what has gone wrong.

Stage 11
Implementation — later phases

Results of first phase used   Specialist departs for fresh
to improve implementation   pastures. Money runs out
of later phases. Staff who   System abandoned.
have worked on first phase
act as trainers and
consultants to colleagues

Stage 12
Final result

Staff have gained new skills   Staff have gained nothing,
and confidence in their own   but have become deeply
system. Basis laid for   suspicious of anything to do
co-operative development   with information systems.
towards integrated   The investment of time and
information system for   money has been wasted. The
all museum activities.   last situation is worse than
                                       the first.

subjective, in contrast to the 'objectivity' of systems and techniques; subjective reactions, however, are an objective factor which those who design systems discount at their peril. This is why Figure 8.1 shows two possible 'plots' alongside the stages of planning and implementation: one representing the kind of action likely to lead to success, and the other the opposite.

For the sake of completeness, the situation of initiating and carrying through large-scale system developments, covering the whole institution, is dealt with. Obviously not all information system developments are of this kind; many are limited to small changes in a single department or section of a department. Whatever the scale, however, the principles are the same, and while evidently some stages can be omitted or telescoped when working on a small scale, it is useful to see the whole sequence.

● Initiatives

Initiatives leading to a decision to set up or improve an information system may arise in part of a museum — in an individual department, for instance — or they may be taken for the museum as a whole, with the museum director taking the first steps.

In the first case, it is important for the person with the idea to do a good deal of preliminary thinking and then introduce it to colleagues (both professional and clerical) in the department so as to test the idea and gain their support. The next stage should be to clear the lines with management; depending on the management structure, this may be simply a matter of reporting that the department plans to do some work on information handling, or it may involve obtaining formal permission. Either way, it is important to keep those to whom one is answerable informed from an early stage. Colleagues in other departments should also be told about the proposed developments; they may have something to gain from them, or ideas to contribute, and they are more likely to start thinking of their own information problems and to join in what may become a total museum information system if they are brought in at an early stage and given the chance of becoming 'founder members'.

If the initiative comes from the top, and covers the whole museum, the same essential of bringing everyone involved into discussion of the idea applies. The keepers of individual departments, together with senior administrative and financial staff, will be the first people to be consulted, and this may well lead to a simple discussion document, setting out the reasons for the initiative and inviting staff to start thinking about information-handling problems and possibilities as they affect their own work, which can be discussed within departments.

● *Introducing specialists*
The situation may be one in which it is clear from the start that specialist advice will be necessary — for example it may be evident that a computerized system will be the appropriate solution because of the size of the collections or because the museum has free access to computer facilities. The ideal situation is the one in which someone *inside* the museum has the necessary expertise; this gives a head start, because a member of staff does not have to spend the same time as an outside specialist in getting to know what happens at present, or in gaining the confidence of staff.

Failing a homegrown expert, the person selected should be someone who has an appreciation of the ways in which museum information-handling problems differ from, say, those of science or commerce, and who above all is able to establish mutual confidence and professional respect with people from other disciplines. He or she must be able to explain the essential concepts involved in computer handling of information in terms that are accessible to people whithout specialized knowledge (and quite possibly with unacknowledged fears and prejudices), and to grasp their explanations of their own specialisms.

The timing of the introduction of an outside specialist is important. It should preferably come at a point when everyone concerned has had a chance to do some thinking on the subject, but before any hard and fast positions have been taken up. This allows the specialist adviser to integrate himself/herself into the whole team at an early stage, and so be able to help the staff to undertake their own analysis and planning.

● Setting up a programme of action

After preliminary consultations and agreement that the initiative towards information system development is worth pursuing, it is necessary to set up a programme of action, with defined responsibilities and a timetable, so as to gain an impetus for the task and establish a business-like way of working. The programme will need to cover the analysis of what happens at present, identifying priority needs, and pinpointing areas of difficulty — as described in Chapter 3. It should set a realistic time target for completion of these activities, and nominate key people responsible for carrying them through and for seeing that everyone concerned participates with full understanding. Informal meetings will need to be built into the programme, so that progress can be checked and ideas exchanged.

● Analysis of the existing system

If a specialist is engaged for the project, he/she will be the right person to help the staff to set about this analysis and to devise ways of recording their findings. Otherwise, the staff will need to undertake this for themselves. The sequence of activities in the summary at the end of Chapter 3 (p38) could form a framework. At this stage, it should be sufficient if a brief statement of the actual situation in relation to each of the questions can be drawn up. Quantitative data can be kept to a minimum. On the policy questions, such as the effects of development plans, input from management will be necessary.

An incidental benefit from examination of what happens at present is that it may of itself suggest some easily made improvements which can be implemented whatever else happens. There may turn out to be two stages of processing that could be merged into one; there might be points where curatorial staff are doing essentially clerical tasks which could without detriment be handled by existing clerical staff whose work would thereby be made more responsible and rewarding; or there may be weak points where a checking stage should be introduced. The general principle should be that people spend as much of their working time as possible exercising their specialized skills, and as little as possible doing things that could be done by people with less specialist skill or knowledge.

● Recommendations, financial resources, overall system pattern

When the existing situation has been analysed and information needs identified by the people most closely concerned, it is possible for them to make some first recommendations about what an information system should accomplish to help their own situation. The recommendations should then be brought together and some conclusions drawn about the overall system characteristics which should be aimed for (as described in Chapter 4).

These will need to be matched against the resources — of people and of money — available, because the only developments which it is feasible to embark on are those for which there are:

— adequate setting-up resources
— guaranteed resources for future years for maintenance and development.

In this context, it is important to look very closely at existing staff resources and in particular to make an 'audit' of skills and knowledge available among staff. It may well be that there is experience and ability going unutilized — for example, experience of computing among curators, or clerical staff who have previously worked in libraries.

The next step is to see how these at present unexploited resources might be put to use in order to meet the identified needs. If, after that, there is still a gap between what is desirable and the staff resources necessary to provide it, it becomes necessary to think in various directions, for example:

1) the possibility of acquiring the necessary expertise and extra time by a new post (unlikely, but worth thinking about)
2) planning to fill a coming vacancy with someone who has the necessary expertise, combined with redeployment of existing staff to give more time (a more promising approach)
3) finding some outside finance for information development, for example from firms or institutions with an interest in the subject area of the museum
4) buying in some expertise from outside to develop a system and train staff
5) in-house or external training for existing staff
6) obtaining finance from agencies such as the Manpower Services Commission to cover the employment for a short period of suitably qualified graduates or school leavers who would otherwise be unemployed*
7) in-house or external training for existing staff.

Only when all the possibilities have been thought through and found not feasible should the decision be taken to sacrifice the desirable to the possible.

This process of deducing system criteria from the preliminary analysis and balancing them against resources to arrive at the outline of a 'best buy' for the particular museum should be a collaborative effort by senior staff and management, with other staff being kept fully informed of progress and decisions.

---

*An example of good management of a team of MSC-funded staff is described in Chapter 9, pp 169—70

The outcome should be an outline plan setting out the main characteristics of the information-handling system, indicating objectives and priorities, and proposing a timetable for the next phases — those of detailed planning and the start of implementation. If an outside specialist is helping, it is during this phase that he/she should start transferring the main responsibility to the regular museum staff.

● Detailed planning

The main tasks at this stage are:
— Decisions about recording, types of catalogues and indexes and other tools for manipulating records to produce the desired outputs, and the appropriate software and hardware (the terms are used here to cover the equipment and the instructions that make it work in both manual and computer systems) which will meet the defined requirements within budget. Chapters 4, 6 and 7 deal with what is entailed in making these decisions
— Producing the necessary working documents in draft form — input forms for recording, master records, work sheets for indexing, etc. An example is shown in Chapter 9, Figure 9.3
— Producing draft versions of tools to aid consistency, like vocabulary lists and thesauri (see Chapter 5)
— Drafting manuals of instructions to help the people who run the system. Figures 8.2 and 8.3 show some examples of system documentation. It is particularly important to have clearly written guidance to the system and its procedures, and the visual presentation should actively aid the user, instead of, as often happens, hindering access by concealing the structure of the content. This is especially important in computer-based systems, where it is all too easy for the documentation to be written by computer specialists for computer specialists, leaving the user from other disciplines floundering in a sea of jargon. Figure 8.4 shows that it *is* possible to produce an intelligible manual for a computer package.
— Establishing outlines for monitoring progress. Any new system should have built into it simple provision for getting feedback on how things are running, so that the users can see, for instance, whether their prediction of how many records could be completed in a working day is being borne out, and can take corrective action if unexpected things are happening. Simple routines like the weekly entering of the number of records input and checked on to standard forms will yield valuable data, without a great deal of extra effort. If provision is not made at this stage for collecting operational data, it will be almost impossible to gain a full picture from the start

Figure 8.2 System documentation: extract from instructions for filling in proforma for system based on use of a word processor

Each Disc (machine-readable magnetic data store) will commence with the name of the particular File of information it contains, e.g. "Birmingham City Museum: The Chase Collection of British Birds Eggs".

The proforma headings are intended to permit entry of all pertinent information on individual specimens within these Files.

The following notes explain the conventions adopted in using the various categories on the proforma (numbered as on proforma)

4 Original Name   This requires the Latin name of Genus and Species in every case (followed by the abbreviation of the author's name if given) exactly as written on the original label or on the earliest surviving label attached to the specimen or if no label is attached then as written in the original collector's register. If such original names include names for subspecies and variety these are also entered with the prefix subsp and var respectively.

Reproduced with the permission of Birmingham City Museum and Art Gallery

Figure 8.3 System documentation: extract from a manual

9.3 Place Index
This index of 5 x 3 cards relates to all objects and to accessioned photographs and photographs represented in the Photograph Index. Any locality association may be noted, and the conventions used in the Photograph Index are also adopted here (see 9.2.1g above).

The county, parish or town is entered on the top right. The classification, class number and standard name are entered below. The photograph accession number and the object accession number, where relevant, are also given.

The index is filed in order of county, parish, town or village etc. Entries relating to Ireland, Scotland and Wales and to foreign countries are filed at the end of the main sequence.

9.4 Copyright Index
This index of 5 x 3 cards gives the name of photograph copyright holders. They are recorded on the top left and addresses below this. Any changes in address are added. Special reproduction conditions, or preferred styles of acknowledgement are also noted. The index is filed in alphabetical order of the name of the copyright holder.

Reproduced with the permission of the Museum of English Rural Life, University of Reading

138

Figure 8.4 System documentation: from a manual for a computer package

MANCHESTER MUSEUM COMPUTER CATALOGUING UNIT

GENERAL NOTES ON CODING

CODING SHEETS SHOULD BE TYPED OR CAREFULLY
HAND—PRINTED.
W A R N I N G: PRINT NEATLY; THE UMRCC DATA—PREP
OPERATORS HAVE BEEN INSTRUCTED TO REJECT A BATCH
OF SHEETS IF ANY ARE DIFFICULT TO READ.

IF HAND—PRINTING, THE FOLLOWING CHARACTERS
M U S T BE WRITTEN THUS:

ONE: 1 EYE: I ESS: S OH: O ZERO:0 ZED: Z
IT IS RECOMMENDED THAT SEVEN IS PRINTED 7

IF IT IS NECESSARY TO DEVIATE FROM THE RELEVANT
CODING SCHEDULE IT IS V I T A L THAT ALL SUCH
VARIATIONS ARE CAREFULLY DOCUMENTED, OTHERWISE
THE INFORMATION COULD BE RENDERED USELESS.

FOREIGN DIPTHONGS SUCH AS U(UMLAUT) AND
O(UMLAUT) SHOULD BE CODED AS UE AND OE, ETC. THE
SCANDINAVIAN O SHOULD BE RENDERED AS OE.

FREQUENTLY RECURRING TERMS MAY BE ASSIGNED
'LOCAL' ABBREVIATIONS, I.E. ABBREVIATIONS THAT ONLY
HOLD FOR A SINGLE BATCH OF DATA. LOCAL
ABBREVIATIONS MUST BE NOTED ON THE BATCH RECORD
SHEET. IF IT IS DESIRED THAT A LOCAL ABBREVIATION
SHOULD BE CONVERTED TO A 'STANDARD' EDIT (I.E. ONE
DONE AUTOMATICALLY BY THE COMPUTER WHEN A BATCH
FILE IS 'STARTED') THE 'ADD' COLUMN ON THE BATCH
RECORD SHEET SHOULD BE TICKED.

UNUSUAL STRINGS OF CHARACTERS SHOULD ALWAYS BE
CHOSEN AS ABBREVIATIONS, OTHERWISE UNWANTED
EXPANSIONS MAY OCCUR IN THE DATA. IT IS SUGGESTED
THAT THE FIRST NON—VOWEL CHARACTER OF THE TERM
IS TAKEN, AND 'X' OR 'Z' ADDED.

E.G. MICROSCOPE = MX OR EGYPTIAN = GZ

MANUAL PAGE A

Reproduced with the permission of the University Museum, Manchester.

of implementation. The consequences of being without such data can be disastrous. Figure 8.5 shows some examples of operational data collected from the Manchester Museum project described in Chapter 9 (pp 169—70).

● Implementation programme

In most situations a phased introduction of new systems is sensible. It allows small groups of people to concentrate their attention on the changeover, rather than the whole staff being involved all at the same time. It allows those concerned to assimilate changes without too much stress. It makes it possible to detect and correct things which are not running properly, and to take account of the lessons in later phases. The risk of loss of data is minimized, and useful outputs can be achieved at an early stage.

Once again, a timetable should be drawn up, with the participation of the people involved, covering:
— the main stages to total implementation, showing their sequence and an estimated timescale
— a detailed timetable for the first stage, with specific time targets, which will be monitored.

● Training

Using the information system should be a thoroughly commonplace activity for everyone concerned with it in any way; it should not be arcane, mysterious, or alarming. The training of the people who will be involved in the pilot stage of implementation is therefore very important. They will, if all goes as it should, be key figures in future developments and an invaluable resource of experience to their colleagues. The amount of time that is needed at this stage for people to grasp the new concepts and master new ways of working so that they feel at ease with them and confident of themselves is often underestimated (a particular case of the general law that everything takes longer than you think it will, and that the excess of actual over expected time is directly proportional to the number of people involved). Skimping on the time for familiarization and training is a false economy. Labour costs are the largest element in the running costs of most organizations, and if the people on whom the system depends are not adequately prepared, not only will the investment in equipment etc be wasted, but their work will not bring any useful return.

Figure 8.5 Operational data collected in the course of implementing a project

Manchester Museum Computer Cataloguing Unit
Six monthly summary of statistics

	No. of cataloguers	Mandays worked *	No. of records prepared	Mean no. of records/ manday
Bird skins	2	208	2742	13.3
Bryozoan microscope slides	1/2**	123.5	3345	27.1
Prehistoric stone implements	4	459	2238	4.88
Liverworts	4	408.5	9432	25.7
Minerals	3/2**	277	4400	22.22
Totals	14	1476	22157	15.01

*   Holidays and sick leave excluded from this figure
** Staff levels changed during period covered

Note: these statistics cover the period 7 5 1979—6 11 1979, and include time devoted to training; performance is therefore likely to be higher in the remaining six months of the current project.

Data supplied by Charles Pettitt, The Museum, University of Manchester and reproduced by permission of the Museum.

A training programme is much easier to set up when the people concerned have been involved from the start in the preparatory work. It then becomes a simple matter of ensuring that they have a clear picture of the interrelation of the various parts of the system, and adequate time to try out the activities in which they will be specializing. It is a good policy to plan the training so that the first people trained can develop as trainers of other colleagues; this can be done by giving them further training over a period — starting with the aspects they need immediately, and going on to broaden and deepen their knowledge of the system so that they can become information resources themselves and can take over the training of their colleagues as new phases are implemented. If an outside specialist is being used, the setting up of the training programme will probably be one of his/her responsibilities.

● Implementation

Once the training is completed and the system documentation is in a working (not a final) state, implementation can begin. If a manual system is being introduced, it should be possible to discontinue the superseded way of working at the same time as the new one is introduced. The records created by the old system should however be retained for use until such time as they have been fully replaced, and nothing should be discarded until a thorough checking process has been gone through. If a computer system is being introduced to replace a manual one, the manual system should go on running until it is quite certain that the computer one is error free and performing to specification.

● Monitoring

Once implementation starts, there should be regular meetings of the team concerned in the pilot phase in order to monitor progress towards targets, discuss ideas for improving procedures, discuss feedback from users of the outputs, decide on the admission of 'candidate terms' to the thesaurus, etc. Such meetings can develop into sessions which lead to creative interactions, such as transactions between team members to develop new refinements to the system or to overcome difficulties, and proposals for system development to meet future needs. They can also lead to initiatives towards other departments, and prepare the way for a completely integrated system to meet all the information requirements of the museum (see Chapter 4, pp 39—42), which is responsive to changing needs. The leader of the team has great opportunities for building up a working group whose members can extend their capabilities and develop confidence in themselves.

If the programme of implementation is a phased one, the cycle of preparation, training, implementation and monitoring is repeated, using feedback from previous cycles, for each phase.

Chapter 9
Case studies: how some museums have dealt with their
information-handling problems

It seemed worth while to end this book with some brief descriptions
of what is actually happening in a selection of museums on the
information front. Comparatively few articles on this topic find a
place in the journals, yet an account of how professional colleagues
have solved problems akin to one's own can sometimes be worth any
amount of theoretical discussion of information concepts. The
museums described have been selected because they illustrate ideas
and approaches discussed in the book, and they have also been
chosen to cover a span of disciplines from hard science to social
history and art, and a range of sizes from the very small to the
national. They all exemplify an analytical approach, solutions related
to needs and to resources, and good management of the most
important resource of all — the human one. There are many others
that could equally well have been used for this purpose, but limits
on the length of the book, and geography (I was to some extent
restricted to museums within easy reach or which lay in directions
I had to visit for other purposes!), made fairly stringent selection
necessary.

The case studies are grouped roughly according to the type of
system involved, running from wholly manual, via various types of
mechanization, to computerized — batched and on-line.

● Manual systems which are likely to remain manual

● *Castle Museum, Norwich, Department of Art*
The Art Department of the Castle Museum at Norwich houses a
major collection of works of the Norwich School, together with
topographical material relating to Norwich and Norfolk. The
collections are used for research by both museum staff and outside
researchers, and the internal research is linked in some instances to
publication. The richness of the topographical collection means that
the material is frequently called on as a source of illustration and
information for many purposes. Users seek pictures which show
particular streets or architectural features, portraits of local worthies,
records of historical events, depictions of various kinds of wildlife,
etc, as well as works by particular artists or in given media.

The main effort by the Keeper and the curatorial staff has therefore been to allow ready access by all these ways, with the maximum economy in recording. The system is a wholly manual one, and is likely to remain so in the present economic situation. Curatorial time is concentrated on the creation of the master record, where professional knowledge is essential, and the derivation of the series of indexes described below is mainly a clerical task (some of it carried out by volunteer workers in the museum).

The way in which the department meets its need for information handling can be most easily set out in a simple flowchart; Figure 9.1 shows this.

It has been found, in the course of several years of operating the system, that only minimal vocabulary control is needed. This is partly because all the indexes and sub-systems are related to the master records, wich are completed by a small number of professional staff who can easily maintain consistency, and partly because the terminology that has been found necessary to meet retrieval needs is straightforward and unambiguous.

The simplicity of the approach makes an interesting comparison with a recently described 'device for the iconographical analysis of art objects' (Couprie 1978). This is in effect a classification which constructs class numbers from an alphanumeric notation in order to represent the content of pictures: 73C 8646, for instance, stands for the Prodigal Son returning to his father, while should an inquirer have need of a picture in which 'a chamber pot is emptied from above' he will find what he requires at 33C 2291.

● *Museum of English Rural Life, Institute of Agricultural History, University of Reading*

The information-handling systems of the Museum of English Rural Life are unusually interesting, in that they are very close to those commonly used in special libraries, and hence rather a-typical for museums.

The collections cover all aspects of agricultural history and rural life, in particular the development of tools, implements and machinery, practical farming, and rural industries. Besides objects, the Institute has a large photographic collection, and a trade record collection. There is also a library of books, pamphlets and periodicals. Documentation, objects, and photographic records are therefore integrated to an unusual extent. For museum objects, the accession form acts as the initial record. This, besides acquisition data, carries classification, description, dimensions, associated information, and bibliographic references. The accession records are filed in accession number order to create one catalogue file.

They are complemented by a classified catalogue file — the 'photograph index'.*This is a card index, whose records consist of data structured in a set sequence:
standard name (ie that used in the index to the classification — see below)
type/design
function/material
method of operation/power/traction
maker
maker's trade mark or specification
location
date
bibliographic or archival reference
copyright holder
accession number

Because the same classification is used for objects and photographs, it is possible to have a combined classified catalogue for them, in which some of the records relate to museum objects, some to photographs in the museum's own photographic collection, and some to photographs in external collections. Figure 9.2 shows the files of records for objects and photographs and their inter-relations. The trade records cannot be accessed in the same way as the object and photograph records because they are classified on a different system and handled according to different procedures.

The main classification, designed originally for museum objects, and then extended to photographs (but not to documentary material), is the essential element of the system for organizing and retrieving information. Most of the classes are activities, eg Harvesting, Processing; others represent object groups like Buildings, concepts like Society, and occupational groups. Within each class there is a hierarchy of two or three sub-divisions, reflected in a numerical notation, for example:
30 CRAFTS
   50 Straw
      10 dollies
      20 hats
      30 rope
      40 skeps
      50 thatch
         10 buildings
         20 rick

---

* As a back-up, there is also a duplicate set of photographed index cards, stored like the original negatives, in accession order.

Figure 9.1 Information-handling systems in the Department of Art, Norwich Castle Museum

Recording	brief description to museum accession book
	master record created by curator, typed by art department staff colour coding used a) to show medium b) to distinguish items from Colman collection
Creation of catalogue	master records filed, alpha by artist's name, within that, by accession no.; biographic record card filed at beginning of records for each artist
Creation of indexes	series of indexes derived from master record by art department staff:
	Norwich topography; alpha by place and subject
	Norfolk topography; alpha by place
	other places in UK and abroad
	features (ie subject content of picutres, eg. arms and armour, gipsy camps, hunting) alpha by subject
	portrait sitters; alpha by name
	gallery index; by location
Creation of supporting sub-systems	historic file: correspondence, information from donor, etc; donor sequence for collections, artist sequence for other material master record is coded to show if there is historic file entry relating to it
	artist file, exhibition catalogues, etc; alpha by name
	photographic file: photographs of items in collections, and of items in other collections by artists represented in museum; separate sequence for major collections (eg Crome), and for other artists; colour coding to indicate which museums hold paintings not in Norwich collections

Figure 9.1 Continued

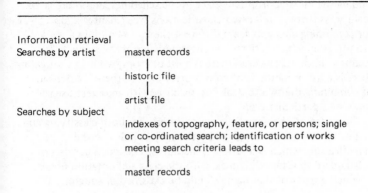

Information retrieval
Searches by artist   master records
                       historic file
                       artist file
Searches by subject
                       indexes of topography, feature, or persons; single
                       or co-ordinated search; identification of works
                       meeting search criteria leads to
                       master records

Figure 9.2 Museum of English Rural Life: information handling for objects and photographs

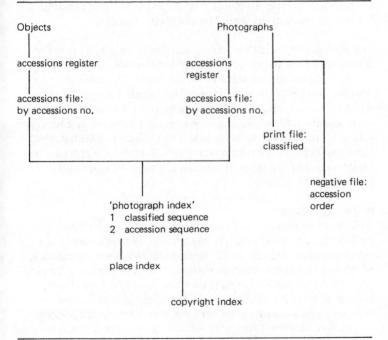

Objects   Photographs

accessions register   accessions
                      register

accessions file: accessions file:
by accessions no.   by accessions no.

                               print file:
                                 classified

                                        negative file:
                                        accession
                   'photograph index'   order
                   1   classified sequence
                   2   accession sequence

                   place index

                        copyright index

147

The classification is not a faceted one; objects are classified by finding the most appropriate place in the schedules, and there is no facility, as there is in faceted classifications (see Chapter 2, pp 15–16), for combining elements from different classes to build up a classification which reflects the characteristics of the subject. For example, in the Crops class there is a list of crops, while in Cultivating there is a list of methods of crop protection, but there is no means of combining the two to deal, for instance, with an object used for spraying a particular crop.

Guidance on the use of the classification, for both classifying and retrieving information, is given by the subject index to the classification, which is in effect a thesaurus. The index consists of:
— 'standard' (preferred) names, with the class and notation under which objects of that name should be classified or sought

— entry terms which lead from non-preferred alternative terms to standard names

— 'subject-related' entry terms, for parts or aspects of subjects, which lead the user to standard terms under which information on these parts or aspects should be classified or sought.

The main starting point for subject searches is the subject index to the classification, to identify the class and notation under which items having the desired features will be found. This takes the searcher into the photograph index, from which it is possible to go direct to relevant objects or photographs, or to the accession records for supplementary details, or to the copyright index. A supplementary way in is provided by the place indexes to objects or photographs; these too lead into the photograph index. Systems and procedures are documented in a series of manuals (Institute of Agricultural History, 1973, 1978).

● *The Rye Museum*
While most of the case studies in this chapter are drawn from medium to large museums, it is important to remember the numerous small and very small museums up and down the country, which serve a valuable purpose with minimal staff resources. In some ways their information-handling problems are the most difficult, because at present — though the situation may change in future — their very smallness cuts them off from help from outside resources.

The Rye Museum (the second of that name — the first was bombed during the Second World War, and was replaced in 1954 by the present one, housed in a tower which is an Ancient Monument, run almost wholly by voluntary effort. It is administered by the Rye

Museum Association, and receives no grant, its income being provided solely by tourists and other visitors to the museum. While display and presentation have been able to benefit from the Honorary Curator's professional experience as an industrial designer, there is no-one with museum training associated with the museum. Despite these difficulties, a consistent policy of recording has been followed, which does allow access to the collections in the ways which are most needed.

Items are entered in an accessions book with an identifying number that contains a coding to show whether they are from the collections of the old museum or have been acquired since the new one was established. Receipts to donors are filed alphabetically by donor name, thus forming a donor index, and purchases are recorded in an inventory book.

A single-sequence card catalogue is built up from records of each object, hand-written in a standard format:
title
provenance and description
bibliographical references to object
size
donor
date
reference number

The catalogue is a classified one — a reasonable decision, since resources do not permit either copying to form multiple sequences or supplementing by indexes. The categories of the classification are based on the content of the collections and on the nature of the subject questions which are put. Thus there are categories for material, eg pottery, which is subdivided as:
Sussex
   Rye
      Named manufacturers,
      in chronological sequence

and for activities, like shipping, where the subdivisions are:
customs and excise
regattas
smuggling
wrecks

Cross references are provided where necessary, for instance between the travel and shipping classes.

● Manual system, based on optical coincidence cards

● *Norfolk Archaeological Unit*
   (now part of the Norfolk Museum Service)
While it is not strictly speaking a museum (although it performs many museum functions in respect of sites and finds, and has close links with the archaeology department of Norwich Castle Museum) the Norfolk Archaeological Unit merits a place in this chapter on account of its very well thought out application of post-coordinate indexing using optical coincidence cards.

   It was necessary to set up a system which allowed access to data about the county's archaeological sites through various characteristics, not only for the benefit of the Unit's own staff and other archaeologists, but also to aid the planning departments of District and County councils in checking what is in and on the ground in areas where building or civil engineering works are proposed.

   Each site is given a unique number (the 'county number') which is allocated from a running sequence; the numbers are also marked on a set of large-scale maps, with colour coding to indicate the size and type of the site. The main system is based on master records which give parish, district, OS sheet reference, and a brief description. They are supplemented by file cards which allow for further details, including site condition, names and addresses of owners and tenants, and details of air photographs (which are held in a separate but linked system), as well as names of museums where finds are held. Some colour coding is used in the primary records to show listed buildings or scheduled ancient monuments. Index terms for sites are assigned on the basis of the content of the records. The terms are entered on a worksheet (Figure 9.3) together with the identifying number of the site. The vocabulary used is controlled; the number of terms in use is not large, and the agreed ones are set out in a combined manual and thesaurus.

   The actual indexing is a matter of extracting the optical coincidence cards headed with the relevant terms, locating them under a co-ordinate drill, and drilling holes through them at the numbered position that corresponds to the record number on the worksheet. The cards are filed in several alphabetical sequences by category, eg parishes, periods, buildings and structure, condition. Searches are made by defining the search query in terms which are used in the thesaurus, taking out the optical coincidence cards which carry those terms, locating them together over a light box, and noting the numbers which are common to all the cards involved in the search — shown by a spot of light shining right through the holes which coincide (see Chapter 6, pp 79, 82). The numbers of these holes represent the master records which meet the search criteria, and the

Figure 9.3 Worksheet for indexing

NORFOLK ARCHAEOLOGICAL UNIT   County Number . . . . .

O.C.D.R. INFORMATION SHEET

Parish:

Period:

Form:

Condition:

Status:

Collections:

Special classification:

Reproduced by permission of the Norfolk Archaeological Unit

next step is to consult them. The system is now being extended to cover finds as well as sites. The worksheet for finds is a checklist of terms drawn up by the county archaeologists, which is ticked by the indexer to indicate which terms should be used. A number of pre-coordinated terms are used, eg there are separate terms for prehistoric pottery, Roman pottery, Middle Saxon pottery, etc, instead of the terms being built up by drilling, for example a card headed 'Roman' and a card headed 'Pottery' to produce an entry for Roman pottery. This degree of pre-coordination is a wise precaution against what is called in library circles 'false drop'. An example shows the dangers. Suppose a search query asked for sites which had yielded both Bronze Age inhumations and Pagan Saxon pottery. Searching on the four separate terms:
1) Bronze Age
2) Inhumations
3) Pagan Saxon
4) Pottery
would produce not only the desired combinations 1 & 2 and 3 & 4, but also the unwanted ones of 1 & 4 and 2 & 3. Discarding the unwanted ones is not much trouble when the number of records retrieved is small, but when it runs to several tens it invalidates the system.

151

The system is in fact beginning to verge on the limits of numbers of records which can conveniently be handled by an optical coincidence system, even with cards allowing for 10,000 numbers. Once the 10,000th record is passed, it becomes necessary to go on to a second card for each feature which has to be indexed after that point, regardless of how full the first card is. The logical next step would in fact be transfer to computer.

● *The Sedgwick Museum, Department of Geology,*
   Cambridge University

The Sedgwick Museum, a major geological research collection, was in a sense the cradle of the GOS package of the MDAU because it was here that the experimental projects which led to the development of GOS were carried out in the period 1967 to 1976.

The Sedgwick was chosen as the site of the project because of the high quality of its manual system of information handling, which dates in the main to the early 1930s, although its origins are Victorian. The main value of the project (described by Cutbill, 1973, and by Porter, Light and Roberts, 1977) lay in the testing of the feasibility of computer production of museum catalogues and indexes, and in the foundation it provided for what is now a very flexible and powerful package.

So far as the Sedgwick Museum itself is concerned, while it proved impossible, on financial grounds, for the project to be carried through to the point of providing all the planned outputs for the whole collection, the Museum nevertheless acquired some useful outputs which continue to be used alongside the manual system, which was, of course, never dismantled. Of particular value is the complete drawer catalogue, which allows checking for inventory and security purposes.

The manual system, described fully by Price (1979) is an unusually comprehensive one; its main features are shown in Figure 9.4. It is worth noting that the card index, while its primary arrangement is taxonomic, is not solely taxonomic; it also gives abbreviated stratigraphical and geographical data for each specimen, together with references to any relevant illustrations, descriptions or citations in the literature.

The collections and their major documentation system are supplemented by the Curators' Library, which consists of annotated publications dealing with Museum specimens, together with collectors' notebooks, maps, original catalogues, and correspondence.

Figure 9.4 Manual documentation system, Sedgwick Museum

accessioning	research	curatorial staff
	identification	
	catalogue number assigned	
preliminary record created	ms catalogue entry prepared	
specimens added to collection	labels prepared: condensed version of catalogue entry colour coded for types, figured specimens, etc	museum assistants
	specimens added to collection at appropriate location: stratigraphical arrangement, sub-divided on geographical and then on broad taxonomic basis	
index entries created	details of specimens added to taxonomic card index: by major taxonomic group, then under taxonomic binomials in alpha sequence; within each taxonomic name by number: colour coding for type and figured specimens	museum assistants
final record created	ms catalogue entry typed and entered in Shelf-catalogue binders: individual entry for each specimen — taxonomic determination, horizon & locality + ownership and research history and bibliographical references	museum assistants
information retrieval — by horizon locality etc	direct from arrangement of specimens (data from specimen labels)	
— by taxonomic data	from card index ——— specimens	
— by individual specimen	shelf catalogue ——— collectors notebooks, original labels, correspondence, etc	
updating records	new/revised catalogue entries, labels, index entries	

● A system based on a word processor

● *Birmingham City Museum, Department of Natural History*
The department has important bird and entomology collections, and
several herbarium collections. They were uncatalogued, and a solution
was sought which would both produce hard copy catalogues and
allow for information retrieval under keywords. The use of a
computer was not feasible on economic grounds, but it proved
possible to meet the requirements by means of a word processor
(essentially, a word processor is a typewriter with a memory: it
creates a record on magnetic tape or disc (as in this case) which can
be edited and corrected, usually on a visual display unit, and into
which instructions can be incorporated for printing out in various
formats). The machine selected (IBM System 6) was a fairly
sophisticated one which allows considerable variation in the forms of
output, and permits easy editing of records.

The other part of the solution was made possible by funding from
the Manpower Services Commission, in the form of a Special
Temporary Employment Programme grant to employ nine young
graduates for a year to prepare records for input, and a typist to
operate the machine.

Before input could start, preliminary work had to be done to
arrive at a suitable format and conventions to guide the people using
it. To start with, the Keeper of Natural History designed a single
proforma which was in effect a checklist including all the data
elements that would be needed for all the collections. From this,
separate forms were derived for each of the three types of specimen.
The forms were then tested for compatibility with word processor
use; some minor modifications proved necessary, but the basic
principle was acceptable.

Conventions for entering data were arrived at through discussions
with the cataloguing teams. It was decided to retain as much as
possible of the original wording, especially in the bird collection
where there were texts of up to half a page of narrative. The details
relating to the data elements of the form would be codified, while
the remaining text would be input in a way that would allow it to be
printed out either as an abbreviated entry or together with the
standard classified record relating to it.

The problem of assigning data to the correct place on the form
was solved by frequent discussions during the first month of
operation which gradually built up a body of precedent, while the
original terminology used by collectors was dealt with by compiling
a list of codewords which provided for using old terms and other
synonyms in their original form as entry terms.

154

The guidance on input was embodied in a brief manual. Data from the completed forms are typed on the word processor; since it can create an ordinary typescript at the same time as a magnetic tape/disc record, the hard copy is used for checking, and corrections are made at the keyboard and again checked on visual display, before it is passed for output.

The primary output is in the form of catalogues in systematic order. It is also possible to produce listings under keywords such as name of collector, habitat or locality. Figure 9.5 shows an example from a locality index. The output is of good enough quality to be used as master for small offset reproduction, and is in this respect superior to computer line printer output.

The work described here is an interesting example of the exploitation of the information-processing possibilities of the word processor to serve museum purposes. There is good potential for more such work in both museums and libraries; to date word processors have tended to be used in office contexts where their full range is not usually explored. Museums are in a good position to develop ways of using their capacity for producing varied outputs from a single input.

● Manual system, supplemented by micro-computer

● *North of England Open Air Museum, Beamish, County Durham*
The museum at Beamish was established in 1971, with the purpose of bringing together on a large parkland site an integrated collection of buildings, industrial plant, agricultural machinery, and items from commercial and domestic life, which would represent the history of all aspects of the life of the North East of England, so far as possible in a 'living' form.

The museum seeks to serve its region by offering enjoyment to the public, educational opportunities for local schools and further education colleges, and research facilities for workers in the field of social history and industrial archaeology.

From the start, the development policy of the museum has included the planning of documentation. Starting from a level of recording which could be consistently maintained by a small nucleus of curatorial and clerical staff, the plan envisaged progress to fuller recording and maximum exploitation of information resources. At an early stage a classification scheme was developed by the museum's director (North of England Open Air Museum, 1980). The scheme, which classifies objects primarily according to original use, has been applied not only for museum specimens but also for the recording of buildings preserved on site and for photographs and general

Figure 9.5 Part of an index produced by word processor

Locality	Grid ref.	Common Name
Byfleet (Surrey)	TQ06	Small Skipper
Byfleet (Surrey)	TQ06	Small Skipper
Byfleet (Surrey)	TQ06	Small Skipper
Byfleet (Surrey)	TQ06	Small Skipper
Byfleet (Surrey)	TQ06	Small Skipper
Byfleet (Surrey)	TQ06	Small Skipper
Byfleet (Surrey)	TQ06	Large Skipper
Byfleet (Surrey)	TQ06	Large Skipper
Byfleet (Surrey)	TQ06	Large Skipper
Chipstead Surrey	TQ25	Dingy Skipper
Chipstead (Surrey)	TQ25	Small Skipper
Chipstead (Surrey)	TQ25	Small Skipper
Chipstead (Surrey)	TQ25	Small Skipper
Chipstead (Surrey)	TQ25	Small Skipper
Chipstead (Surrey)	TQ25	Small Skipper
Chipstead (Surrey)	TQ25	Small Skipper
Chipstead (Surrey)	TQ25	Large Skipper
Chipstead (Surrey)	TQ25	Dingy Skipper
Chipstead (Surrey)	TQ25	Dingy Skipper
Chipstead (Surrey)	TQ25	Dingy Skipper
Chipstead (Surrey)	TQ25	Dingy Skipper
Chipstead (Surrey)	TQ25	Dingy Skipper

156

information. An interesting feature is the use of the Standard Industrial Classification for the Industries section of the classification.

The development of the classification scheme made it possible to provide a subject way in to the records from quite an early point, and the existence of a classification will form the basis for future refinement of this approach. There are at present two main sets of records: the general file which covers museum objects and buildings, and the photographic file. The sequences in which they are arranged are similar, and both make use of the classification for subject arrangement. The flow chart of Figure 9.6 shows how the system works.

A thesaurus is planned, and a recently acquired micro-computer (an Apple) linked with a word processor will be used in experiments on information retrieval — allowing searches to be made on accession number, classification, and keywords. The computer will also be used for museum accounting and statistical purposes, and an experimental program for this purpose has been written in-house, in BASIC.

This is an interesting and unusual example of a museum tackling computerized information handling on its own — having first defined and met its main requirements by a manual system.

● Manual system, with plans for progressing to
   computer + microforms

● *The Wellcome Museum at the Science Museum, London*
The transfer to the Science Museum of the large collections of the Wellcome Trustees (with the exception of the Wellcome Library and museum of pathological specimens, which remain in their former location in the Wellcome Institute) has provided the opportunity for analysis and system planning which should ultimately benefit the whole of the Science Museum (this is an example of the type of situation discussed in Chapter 4, p55).

The conditions for an integrated consideration of all information systems have been created by the fact that one member of the Museum's staff, based on the Science Museum Library, has overall responsibility for information systems development throughout the Museum and its Library. The Wellcome collection consists of more than 150,000 objects in the field of medical history, broadly interpreted. Among the first problems of the transfer of such a large collection was that of establishing foolproof methods of physical control. A detailed flow chart was prepared showing each stage of the processing for objects, from unpacking and cleaning, extraction of related documentation, assigning of accession numbers, catalogue

Figure 9.6 Information-handling systems,
North of England Open Air Museum, Beamish

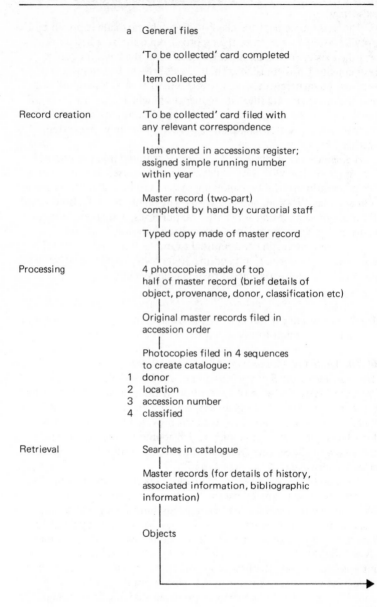

a General files

    'To be collected' card completed

    Item collected

Record creation   'To be collected' card filed with
any relevant correspondence

    Item entered in accessions register;
assigned simple running number
within year

    Master record (two-part)
completed by hand by curatorial staff

    Typed copy made of master record

Processing   4 photocopies made of top
half of master record (brief details of
object, provenance, donor, classification etc)

    Original master records filed in
accession order

    Photocopies filed in 4 sequences
to create catalogue:
1 donor
2 location
3 accession number
4 classified

Retrieval   Searches in catalogue

    Master records (for details of history,
associated information, bibliographic
information)

    Objects

Figure 9.6 continued

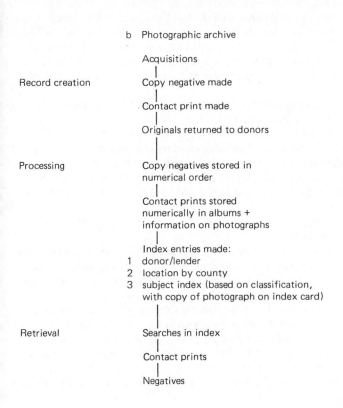

b   Photographic archive

Acquisitions

Record creation   Copy negative made

                         Contact print made

                         Originals returned to donors

Processing   Copy negatives stored in
                         numerical order

                         Contact prints stored
                         numerically in albums +
                         information on photographs

                         Index entries made:
                       1 donor/lender
                       2 location by county
                       3 subject index (based on classification,
                         with copy of photograph on index card)

Retrieval   Searches in index

                         Contact prints

                         Negatives

card preparation, photographing of each object, through to filing
of catalogue cards and entry of photographs into pictorial
identification books.

Checking procedures are included at each stage to ensure control,
and some of the details are ingenious and well thought out: for
example, where new accession numbers have to be assigned (the
original number is used if it is findable, but in many cases it is not)
pre-printed labels are used to ensure that each object is given a
unique number, and when the photographs are taken, the scale of
the object is shown by inclusion in the picture of a card cut-out of
a standard size (indicated by distinctive shape) with the object's
accession number written on it.

The subject areas of the collection present many problems of terminology, because of the existence of alternative, variant and local names. As with other collections of this kind, the concept of 'simple name' and 'full name' is giving difficulty (see MacKie, 1978). It has been found necessary to construct an outline classification and to start compiling a thesaurus — the first part of which is a broad subject grouping which is being used for ordering the subject file of records.

The main sequence of records is filed by accession number; a supporting sequence is made by photocopying the master records and the photocopies are filed by subject. Problems of storage space are arising, and the solution being considered is that of making a microfilm record for the subject sequence, which could be fed into fiche jackets. A computer system is seen as the ultimate objective — not just for the Wellcome material, but for the Science Museum and Library as a whole.

At present, various alternatives are being considered. The possibilities include:
— using the GOS programs, and processing on the Cambridge computer
— acquiring a mini-computer for the Science Museum, which could be used not only for museum and library information retrieval, but also for administration and house-keeping routines.

On the software side, as well as the GOS package, other possible options under consideration are the adaptation of the MARC software designed for library data processing to handle museum as well as library data, and/or the use of standard information retrieval packages, such as MINISIS, STATUS, CAIRS, FACTFINDER or ASSASSIN (details of suppliers are listed at the end of the bibliography on p184.

The economics of information handling as between the production of printed indexes and listings on the one hand and on-line interactive search on the other, are also being studied as part of system design. It will probably be necessary, on grounds of accessibility and security, to produce printed or microfiche (COM) output of the most commonly used catalogue sequences.

● MDAU pilot schemes, using GOS

● *St Albans Museums*
The first public museum in St Albans, the City Museum, opened in 1898. It did not have a formal catalogue, and an accessions register was begun only in the 1950s. The Verulamium Museum was opened in 1939, essentially as a museum on the site of the Roman town, to house the finds from the excavations by Sir Mortimer Wheeler and

Kathleen Kenyon, to which were added finds from Professor Frere's excavation of 1955—61. The two museums are now administered by St Albans District Council.

The only documentation for the Verulamium museum was a rough card index, with one or more cards being prepared for each object as it came into the museum. There was no accessions procedure, and the cards were of limited use, even when taken in conjunction with the relevant excavation notebooks.

When the present Keeper of Documentation joined the staff of the museum in 1976, she was engaged in work for the Field Department, writing up the results of the more recent excavations. When she wanted to search the records for parallels, it was difficult to find relevant material, because they were not indexed, everything was still grouped as it had come out of the ground.

A start was made in 1977 on tackling the documentation problems, with an examination of the feasibility of using the MDA system. The permanent appointment of a Keeper of Documentation (still an unusual job title in museums) in 1979 allowed a consistent programme of work to start. The feasibility study led to a decision to use MDA cards. These form the master record; no accessions register is kept. The catalogue is created from a single sequence of the cards in accession number order (the accession number is a simple, non-significant one, reflecting only date of registration). It is planned to copy the catalogue on to microfiche for security. The degree of detail to which the MDA cards are filled in has been deliberately kept to a non-intensive level, so as not to overtax staff resources. This leaves the possibility of going over to more intensive recording later, and applying this retrospectively, when resources allow, to the older records.

Another plan for the future is an experiment with using MDA cards as an initial on-site record, to which more details can be added later in the museum, so that a single record is used throughout, without transcription from a site record to a final museum record.

The museum was fortunate in being able to set up a pilot project with the MDAU. This involved a computer-produced catalogue and computer-produced indexes derived from the original master records on the MDA cards. A catalogue was produced for the first 2000 objects catalogued in 1978, and an experimental index has been printed out for the first 500 records catalogued.

The index consists of ten sequences, each arranged according to a different element of information and within that element by a hierarchy of other elements — the typical format of GOS indexes. Figure 9.7 shows the sequences, and Figure 9.8 gives an example from one of the indexes.

Figure 9.7 Index sequences produced by MDA GOS program for St Albans Museum

---

1 Period
    material
        object
            simple name

2 Material
    simple name
        full name

3 Store
    simple name (for audit purposes)

4 Site (by insula and buildings within insula to allow
    correlation between different excavations)
        simple name
            material

5 Simple name
    material

6 Excavator
    material
        simple name (equivalent of donor index)

7 Valuation (restricted information)
    simple name

8 Context period or date (research-oriented index)
    simple name

9 Publication reference (relating illustrations from publications to
                accession numbers)
    accession number

10 Laboratory number (giving access to laboratory records of
                conservation treatment)
    accession number

Figure 9.8 Verulamium Museum: computer-produced index to sites

```
INSULA VI
VER BLDG. 2
  pin bone                       SABMS 78/373  *
  pin bronze                     SABMS 78/409  *
INSULA VII
VER TRIANGULAR TEMPLE
  bead glass                     SABMS 78/480  *
  bead paste                     SABMS 78/482  *
  bracelet shale                 SABMS 78/439  *
  brooch bronze                  SABMS 78/965  *
  chimney earthenware            SABMS 78/430  *
  counter glass                  SABMS 78/3    *
                                 SABMS 78/48   *
```

Reproduced with permission of Verulamium Museum

Most information searches are to answer feature-type questions, and the indexes are planned for this kind of use. Given that at present the record cards are not completed in great detail, it is anticipated that users are likely to go direct from the indexes to relevant objects. The storage of objects is therefore designed to meet as far as possible the search needs. Arrangement is by material, and within that by type of object.

The museum hopes to go on using the MDA system beyond the pilot stage, through a centralized data-processing agency specializing in museum d-p. It is also planned to microfilm the computer-produced index on COM-fiche. Copies could then be deposited in university archaeology departments and other bona-fide research institutions, together with fiche of the catalogue.

The Keeper of Documentation has produced a guide which covers the use of conventions for completing MDA cards, vocabulary control, and a list of keywords which it is hoped to develop into a thesaurus. A discussion group has been set up on archaeological terminology in this connection.

The decision to use computerized information handling was taken because the collections were generating large amounts of information to which access was needed in multiple and detailed ways, while staff resources were limited. The results so far have justified the decision. Staff have gained an increased knowledge of the collections; storage and conservation practice have been upgraded. If the work continues on the same lines, it should lead to fuller realization of the research potential of the museum, as well as to improvements in display, exhibitions, and inquiries and publications services (Stone, 1978, 1979).

● *The Hunterian Museum, Glasgow*
The archaeology and ethnography collections of the Hunterian Museum have been the subject of a MDA project similar to the one just described. In this case study, attention will be concentrated, not on the inputs and outputs, which, given the difference in subject matter, are comparable to those described for Verulamium, but on developments initiated by the museum staff to enable them to get the best out of the MDA system. The thinking which led to these developments has been explained by the Assistant Keeper for Archaeology and Anthropology, who is responsible for the project (MacKie 1978a, b). His account is of particular interest because it shows how a group of cataloguers, in seeking to meet the strict recording criteria necessary for completing MDA cards, were 'forced . . . to devise progressively more systematic lists of approved

terms which can be applied uniformly to artifacts in every branch of museum work which deals with the relics of pre- and non-Industrial societies'.

The first stage in this process was the decision not to make any significant distinction between ethnographic, archaeological and historical material. This led to the realization that for this purpose it would be necessary to have an agreed list of generalized terms which could be used for all objects of the same kind, whatever the collection they belonged to, together with lists of more specific terms for artefacts coming within the scope of each generalized term.

So far they were simply developing their interpretation of the MDA's 'simple name' and 'full name' categories which are used on all MDA cards, but the next step took them a good deal further. The museum staff came to realize that they needed a structured listing, ordered by some principle other than the alphabet, and bringing like things into larger and more general groupings — in fact a classification (cf the discussion of classification in Chapter 2, pp 12–21). The nature of the collections made the only logical basis for grouping that of function, and so the outline of a classification scheme was produced. Its main elements are listed in Figure 9.9. Within each major category, there is a hierarchical listing of 'simple names' and their subdivisions, and within the simple name subdivisions there is a further listing of full names and their subdivisions. This classification is complemented by an alpha list of full names. The classification has a simple numerical notation, confined to a consecutive numbering of the main classes only. It is used, in creating the MDA records, by putting the notation for the appropriate main class after the Simple Name entry. This makes it possible for the computer to produce listings of all objects having the same classification.

Where objects would be relevant in a search for more than one category, the notation for the appropriate main classes, rather than a single main class, can be given in the record. The next stage in the process could well be to extend the vocabulary control from names to other keywords, so as to produce a full thesaurus to complement the classification.

The MDAU, in the manuals it produces for completion of its various cards, includes a recommendation on the lines 'We also suggest that you adopt INTERNAL CONVENTIONS'. It is encouraging to have an example of this suggestion being taken up in a fundamental manner, by a museum which has found benefit from doing so:

'It also has the great advantage of obliging curators — and researchers — working on museum material — to consider their artifacts in terms of their function instead of simply as objects to be classified in

Figure 9.9 Hunterian Museum classification — major categories

1	Tools	implements for manufacturing things
2	Equipment	implements for doing specific things
3	Structures	all buildings for human & animal use
4	Weapons	everything for warfare and hunting
5	Containers	objects for containing other things
6	Holders & supports	for securing things in place
7	Furniture	moveable things for inside buildings
8	Transport	all kinds except extensions of limbs
9	Fabric	every kind except clothing
10	Clothing	everything worn, including footwear and headgear
11	Representations	3-dimensional copies of things
12	Decorations & art	everything decorative except personal
13	Communication & symbols	all forms of writing, etc
14	Ideology & ceremonial	everything ceremonial, religious or not
15	Games & pastimes	all kinds, field and board
16	Fauna	animal remains, unworked or unspecific
17	Flora	palnt remains, unworked or unspecific
18	Mineral	stone & metal, unworked or unspecific
19	Palaeolithic and mesolithic	all implements produced by prehistoric cultures of this type
20	Industrial manufacture	
21	Engines	

typological terms. The benefits to archaeology and museology of this philosophical approach of trying to set artifacts within the framework of functioning human societies are agreed to be great.' (MacKie, 1978a).

● Independent systems, using GOS package

● *British Museum, Ethnography Department*
This example is included, not because it is an operating solution (at the time of writing implementation is just starting), but because it exemplifies the preliminary investigation and planning involved in a systems analysis approach to large-scale information problems. The Ethnography Department was selected as the first department of the British Museum to be studied in this way, to allow a decision to be made on the feasibility of introducing a computerized information retrieval system. One decision taken at an early stage was that the process should not start — as some other computerization experiments elsewhere have started — with wholesale conversion of all existing records into computer form. Such a step would be excessively expensive, time consuming, slow in yielding useable outputs, and liable to be overtaken by changes in technology. Instead, a phased approach was envisaged.

The first phase would consist of extracting from the registers a limited number of information categories for each object — for example, country of origin and name — so as to build a computer file of records, from which typological and geographical indexes could be derived, and on which a simple information retrieval system could operate.

In the next, intermediate, phase, information from sources other than the registers could be added to the basic records, for example, linking records of objects with the photographs of them, thus allowing indexes with cross references to the picture collection. The final phase would see the production of comprehensive records, allowing sophisticated information retrieval. The comprehensive recording could be introduced with new acquisitions, and then extended back into the earlier records as opportunity offered, for example as a by-product of research or of exhibition planning.

The advantages of the phased approach were seen to lie in:
— allowing the initial data extraction to be done by inexperienced graduate staff, with subject help from senior museum staff
— yielding useful output in a comparatively short time

167

— offering flexibility in respect of future technological developments, in that it would be cheaper to make changes in the structure with a phased programme than with a programme where all the lines had been set for several decades
— conferring the economic advantage of being able to make choices at each stage in the light of circumstances at the time
— allowing the use of a batch system in early stages, with the possibility of moving to the more expensive on-line operation when the need arises.

The system design envisages use of a mini-computer already in the Department's research laboratory (Hewlett-Packard 2100) with back-up from external facilities (Civil Service or bureau) for sorting and printing. In the longer term, transfer to a larger machine is proposed.

An existing package is recommended rather than producing a purpose-built set of programs, and the GOS package is considered the best for the initial stages. It can run on a mini-computer, it is designed for museums, and it is flexible — it is especially easy to re-define the record structure. It can handle the complexities of ethnographic information, and is the package most likely to be used by other museums. These advantages outweigh the disadvantages, which lie in the fact that its retrieval procedures are rather limited compared with those of some other packages, that it is batched mode only, and that at present it tends to be computer- rather than user-oriented, lacking explanatory documentation designed for the lay user without special knowledge of computers.

For the preparation of data, a small informal team within the department is proposed. It is suggested that data entry, too, should if possible be carried out by the information team, using a keyboard with a VDU to allow on-the-spot checking, rather than having it key-punched by a typist.

The master file will be on magnetic tape in registration number order. The basic record will contain selected information fields, including registration number together with acquisition details, and object or part details, including name and material, and storage location details. Other information to be held on the computer will include details of the geographical areas for which the Assistant Keepers are responsible, so that indexes can be produced for each Assistant Keeper's area. Long-term, it is also planned to hold thesauri and lexicons on computer.

At the end of the first phase, it is planned to produce on microfilm three comprehensive indexes to the registers: geographical, typological within administrative areas, and global typological. There will also be a facility for ad hoc information retrieval.

168

● *Manchester Museum Computer Cataloguing Unit*

The work of the Unit is worth describing on two counts: the successful use of a program package originally designed for handling bibliographic information, and the equally successful management of a large team of graduates funded by the Manpower Services Commission on a one-year employment project.

The pilot venture was the cataloguing in 1977/78 of the Spence mollusc collection. Since the Museum is part of Manchester University, it was able to use the facilities of the University of Manchester Regional Computing Centre without charge. The decision to use a package intended for dealing with information contained in such documents as periodical articles was taken because it was available, and the format of the package (FAMULUS, which originated from the US Department of Agriculture) could be kept compatible with that of the GOS package which was at that point not yet available. The project was started and supervised by a member of the Museum's staff who had some computing experience combined with subject knowledge; the work was done with the help of one junior and one graduate technician on an 18-month contract under the Manpower Services Commission Job Creation Project scheme. The output from the project was published in the form of a catalogue arranged in taxonomic order to family level and alpha by genus within families, each catalogue record being identified by a simple running number. The catalogue is supplemented by a series of indexes: genera and sub-genera, species, names associated with specimens, etc.

The success of the initial project made it possible to go on to a major enterprise, again funded by the MSC, this time under the Special Temporary Employment Programme. The object was the cataloguing of records in egyptology, archaeology, zoology (including entomology), botany and geology — a total of about 60,000 records. At the time of writing, three subject areas have been completed, and projects are still running in six others (flints, birds, minerals, bryozoa, liverworts and entomology site data).

The setting up and management of the project has been very carefully thought out with a view to ensuring that:
1) the museum's curatorial staff are involved in planning the projects and in providing inputs of subject knowledge to the MSC teams
2) the contribution of the MSC-funded graduates — some of whom are qualified in non-scientific fields — is used as fully as possible, and that they should gain useful skills and experience of the obligations, disciplines and rewards of working life.

The organizational set-up consists of the project supervisor (a member of the permanent staff), a project manager (one of the MSC graduates), a project secretary (MSC graduate), who also deals with entomology site data, and five teams of MSC graduates. While it is necessary, because of the amount of evaluation and decision making involved, to use subject specialists for minerals and flints, it has proved possible for non-specialists to deal with, and indeed become interested in, the other fields, given access to subject advice from curators.

The use of MSC-sponsored graduates and of the computer has demanded a re-thinking by museum staff of ways of working. They have had to move away from the traditional repetition of a complete cycle of activities for the recording of each specimen, and towards the performing of single activities for a large group of specimens which can be carried out by non-specialists, followed by input to the computer, the output from which can be checked by curators while the MSC teams input more data. It has also been found that operations involving look-up of data from other sources are best performed by curators, working with indexed listings of large batches of data. Very simple computer-produced coding sheets are used; it was found that MDA cards caused difficulties for key-punch operators. The results have been gratifying; all the subject specialists are satisfied with the quality of the records produced and some are becoming keenly interested in further possibilities of computer exploitation in their own fields; the teams have been able to work to specific output targets and to take some responsibility for administering their own work; and some of the MSC-funded graduates have got jobs on the strength of their experience on the project.

The scheme has been arranged to yield as much operational information as possible, including average length of records, number of records coded per man-day, manhours required for card punching, amount of computer terminal occupation required for editing, and the amount of processing power required to produce catalogues (some preliminary statistics are quoted in Chapter 8, p141).

Work is now in progress to implement GOS at the museum, with funding from the N W Museum and Art Gallery Service, and in consultation with the Museum Documentation Association. It is hoped that further MSC funding may be available for data input, possibly through Project-based Work Experience, which would involve less-qualified and younger people.

● *National Maritime Museum*
The National Maritime Museum at Greenwich is a national collection which is very intensively used by both public and researchers (a survey of users in 1977 showed that there were 16,000 public inquiries per year reaching curatorial staff).

Established in the 1930s, the museum brought together a number of collections, some of which had their own catalogues compiled by the original owners. Initially, the new museum maintained a central registry, but after wartime staff shortage this was superseded, on O & M advice, by departmental recording, with each department developing its own systems to meet its own needs and with no active attempt to preserve common ground between the ways in which different departments managed matters of documentation.

In 1971, as part of planned development, more attention began to be paid to documentation. As a first step towards bringing together related information which was distributed among the records of various departments, a general information index on cards was set up. The information it contained was derived from the records of the various departments of the museum, and by 1975 it had grown to a size which threatened to become unmanageable.

In 1976, someone who had worked on what became the GOS program package was appointed as Information Retrieval Officer, and towards the end of that year the decision was taken to move towards integrating the whole of the museum's information processing through a computer-based system.

The problems he faced were of a kind that could be expected in a large collection where separate paths had been followed in different departments. A department with 75,000 items, for instance, had none of them numbered. Each had a typed slip with a description, which gave location details, but no acquisition data — this was a deliberate policy to keep things simple. The variety of numbering systems in use included some quite idiosyncratic ones. There were also multiple files on certain categories of item, the files being constructed on different principles and containing different types of information: for instance there were 43 separate files containing records on named ships. The general information index, which had been instituted to overcome some of these problems, was itself in a sense a victim of them, because its data were derived from other files which lacked consistency among themselves, and many of which contained incomplete data.

A clear indication of the cost of these difficulties in gaining access to information came from the survey mentioned above, which indicated that 30—40 per cent of the task of dealing with public inquiries could have been done by less-qualified staff. Many of the inquiries were of a kind that could have been dealt with by reference to suitable museum booklets and other publications, but such aids could not be produced because the means of access to the information needed to compile them was lacking, and the staff were too busy to rectify this.

An initial study of the whole of the existing system was made, with particular attention to the use of staff resources. The decision emerging from this study was that a phased programme, bringing information handling under control in stages, was the appropriate policy. A five-year development plan was drawn up; at the end of that time the system should be operational and all departments included in it. The GOS package would be used for data handling.

Master records are being created within each department, based on MDA conventions. This should mean that the same type of statement will be used on all records, so that where information on a given subject — for example on a named ship — occurs in different departmental records it will be treated in the same way on all. In meeting the requirement that each item recorded should have its own unique number, so far as possible the existing systems of different collections are being adapted; where this is not possible, simple running numbers are being assigned.

Data are entered by departments on mini computers in the museum, and then transferred to the mainframe computer. To date, various indexes have been produced in certain departments. In the department of manuscripts, for instance, a series of indexes has been produced to the collection of some 1200 handwritten documents by Nelson. They are in the form of listings by given elements of information from the master record, such as date, recipient, bibliographic form etc (the last-named listing revealed the existence, hitherto unknown, of four codicils to Nelson's will). Another useful development has been the production of a computer catalogue to the museum's library, which is classified by UDC.

The principle adopted in putting data on to computer is that all the elements which need to be manipulated to produce various information outputs should be put on. Other supplementary data can be dealt with by Xerox reproduction, or by putting on to microfiche.

The production of multiple listings under various data elements, initially for individual departments and later for similar material held in several departments, will permit many ways in to the records, and will allow the answering of feature and item questions at various levels of specificity.

At the present stage, the foundations are still being laid, and the first benefits are in the consistency of inputs and the development of agreed conventions for recording, applicable across all departments. It is of great value that the co-ordinator of the process is a member of the museum's staff with expert knowledge of computing,

172

particularly of the programs which are being used, who has been able to develop relations of mutual professional respect with his colleagues. He has been able to explain the potential of the GOS programs to them, and they have been able to explain to him the nature of their data and their information requirements. The applications are therefore designed to give optimum service to the needs of curators as defined by themselves — the better the degree of understanding, the better will be the solution.

The preliminary analysis of the museum's information needs started with a consideration of manpower utilization. Implementation of the system should make it possible for the specialist skills and knowledge of the curators to be used for the maximum amount of time at the highest level. Quick and flexible access to the whole resources of the collections will open up possibilities for full exploitation of research potential. At the same time, it will become possible to exploit information resources to create supporting programmes of publication so that staff time does not have to be spent on repeatedly re-assembling information in response to public inquiries on similar topics. This will not mean that curators will be able to retreat behind their office doors and never see a member of the public again; rather they should be freed to make their relations with the public more productive and less routine.

● Computer system, using programs specially produced for the museum

● *Brighton museums*
Brighton is as rich in museums as in other delights. The methods of recording were as diverse as the content of the collections when, in 1974, the Borough Council, which has responsibility for the museums, decided to put museum records on to its ICL System 4 computer, and to design its own system and programs, rather than to wait until the MDA package then under development became available.

The aim of the system, as described by Kirk (1979), was that it should be open-ended and flexible, capable of use by people from various disciplines, and fit to last a long time without substantial modification.

By good fortune, at the time when these developments were being decided on, a curator joined the museum who had worked on the development of a computer record system for geological information for an international oil company. He was able to produce the specification for the system, on the basis of which the Borough Council computer specialist produced the basic programs, and to form the bridge, as project leader, between curators and computer staff. Advice was also forthcoming from the Natural History Museum on appropriate data fields for the natural history collections.

The format for data is a simple one. It consists of two parts: the unique accession number by which each item is identified, and the data-type code, which labels each data element in the record. Each data element is represented by a five-character numerical code; the first four digits stand for the subject and the fifth for sub-subject.

The data are entered by curatorial staff on standard forms; alongside the accession number and the data-type code, they enter the relevant descriptors. They are free to decide on the volume of information entered for any data element up to quite a large limit. Input of data to the computer is batched; all data are checked before input by a designated curator who has this responsibility for each file, and is also responsible for checking output. Outputs consist of:
— an accessions register of new additions from every batch of input
— a serial catalogue, produced every six months, arranged for every collection by accession number, with the data-type codes converted to titles which are followed by the descriptors for each item; the catalogue is produced on COM-fiche
— indexes, produced on request, under any single data element (eg name, case, or label copy); the form of these is keyword, followed by accession numbers of relevant items. There is also a 'compound index' facility (similar to GOS indexes) which permits the production of indexes showing up to five data types in hierarchic sequence
— answers to co-ordinate searches using Boolean logic on combinations of keywords specified by users.

The computer features of the system are straightforward. The programming language is COBOL (a choice arising from the fact of its use for local government purposes by Brighton Council, and a unique one for museum applications). Input is from keyboards with VDUs to disk, from which it is automatically written on to the magnetic tape store of the main computer.

The Brighton system is a particularly interesting one, in that it shows how a group of museums have been able to take advantage of access to a central computer system designed for very different purposes. An important condition for success has been the presence on the curatorial staff of someone with a foot in both the computer and museum camps, who has been able to explain museum problems to computer specialists, and to help his museum colleagues understand how they can exploit the potential of a computer system to meet the needs which they identify from their professional knowledge.

● *Imperial War Museum*

The information-handling system of the Imperial War Museum is particularly interesting as an example of the use of a computer and microforms for the management of a unique film and sound archive. While the responsibilities of the museum's information retrieval department extend to all the collections, including objects and pictures, library and documentary archives, and photographs, it was essential to concentrate first of all on the films because of the deterioration problems associated with nitrate film stock. The two main groupings of films — from the first and second World Wars — were shot on this stock, and it was necessary to find a means of using data about the condition of the films in order to give guidance on the priorities for testing so that preservation work could be carried out on those most in need of it.

In 1974 it became possible to embark on a computer-based system for this purpose (using the Department of Education and Science ICL 1906A computer). As no existing program packages were suitable, a package was specially designed; the opportunity was taken to incorporate a cataloguing sub-system as well as the sub-system for handling technical archive data which was the initial raison d'être of the initiative. Development of the programs, known as APPARAT (Archive Preservation Programme and Retrieval by Automated Techniques) was completed in 1975 and the programs became operational at the end of that year.

The output from the technical data system consists of regular reports and monthly test schedules listing those films due for retesting. The cataloguing sub-system produces a full catalogue, by museum reference number, of all the 'bibliographic' information about films and/or sound recordings so far input to the system (it is possible to input data by stages — minimal information on acquisition, for instance, with subsequent addition of full details or updating). The catalogue is supplemented by indexes of credits (people concerned with the films) and of titles. These are printed-out indexes; there is also a facility for getting ad hoc listings to meet specific inquiries, using AND, OR and NOT logic.

A related feature of the system is the well-developed use of microforms. COMfiche is used for the production of the catalogue and indexes, and for the reference reports from the technical data system (there is also the possibility of using computer typesetting to produce printed catalogues, but so far it has not proved feasible to exploit this). At the same time, the documents related to the films — all the documentation for the second World War films, including the cameramen's 'dope sheets' — is filmed by an agency on 16mm stock and made up into 'fiche jackets'. It is thus possible to refer easily to and fro between the main film catalogue and the fiche reproductions of the related documentation. The NMI fiche readers in use in the museum give very good quality reproduction. Plans for future exploitation include a venture into 'on-demand publishing' — as a first step, it is hoped to market a booklet, which might be commercially printed or produced in-house in the Museum's small offset printshop, with a brief description of a part of the holdings (eg a newsreel series) and a copy of the fiche version of the appropriate part of the catalogue in a pocket inside the back cover.

As well as running its own program package, the museum is also involved in two pilot schemes with the GOS package, dealing with collections of firearms and medals. These projects may lead to the resolution of the at present un-decided question of vocabulary control for subject indexing. The probable outcome is that certain areas of the Museum Documentation Standard will be governed by museum-wide conventions, while vocabulary in other areas will be standardized by subject departments. The system has been described by Smither (1975 and 1979).

● On-line computer system

● *The Hancock Museum, University of Newcastle upon Tyne*
The Hancock is a scientific museum established in the nineteenth century. It now forms part of the University, and the fact that it thereby has access to the University computer has conditioned its choice of solutions to its information requirements.

The choice of computer package was also influenced by the museum's link with the university computer. The SPIRES (Stanford Public Information Retrieval System) package is used by the university, so it was a logical step to try it for handling museum data. In contrast to the GOS package whose use in various museums has been decribed earlier, and which is designed for batched off-line processing, SPIRES is an interactive on-line system (though it can of course be used off-line in batched mode).

The other factor which made it possible for the museum to undertake the developments described below has been the availability of funds from the Manpower Services Commission under the Job Creation Programme and more recently the Special Temporary Employment Programme; this has allowed the museum to employ graduates with appropriate degree subjects for short periods to handle the preparation of data.

Access to information has in the past been hampered by the fact that only some of the material is fully catalogued; other important collections are uncatalogued. When the decision was taken to input data to the university computer, the pilot work was carried out on two collections which were already catalogued: geology (fossils, minerals and rocks) and bird skins. So far the geological collection has been almost completely input (19,000 records) and the 4000 bird records have also been input. More recently, files on lepidoptera records, mammal skins and mammal site records, palaeobotanical slides, and transparencies have been created.

The data about specimens were input from standard forms, completed manually. The data elements in the records under which searches can be made include:

for all records	accession number, name, geographical location of collection
for fossils	phylum
for minerals	chemical formula
for rocks	associated form names, horizon, period
for bird skins	sex, weight, dimension, common and Latin name

There is some control of the vocabulary used in recording; provision is made, for example, for reference from synonyms and old names of fossils to modern terminology.

Data entry is by key punching in the museum; it is checked by curators before being input to the computer, or edited in the active file at a later date.

All the records created so far are held on-line in the university computer. They are accessed from a terminal in the museum. The SPIRES programs allow on-line interactive search, using Boolean logic. Before the computer starts printing out records which meet the search criteria, it is possible to ask it to print out the number of records in which any given descriptor or combination of descriptors occurs. This is a useful facility, because it allows the searcher to modify the search criteria, either by making them more precise if the number of records meeting the original criteria is too large, or by broadening them if there are no records which meet the original criteria. Figure 9.10 shows an example of a search print out. The system can be used to produce a variety of listings as well as for *ad hoc* on-line searches. A collectors' index for all local museums is being produced, as is a catalogue of type and figured specimens of fossils and a complete donor list.

The useful results from the first stages have made it feasible to go on to other collections in the museum; in the next stage the uncatalogued collections, such as the anthropology material, will be brought in.

Figure 9.10 Hancock Museum: search print-out in response to a request to find all fossil records which contain the string of characters 'ORNA'

```
-Spires 5.0
-Tracing on, 'EXPLAIN TRACING' for details
-?) SET NOTRACE
-?) SET LEN 255
-?) SELECT GEOL. COLLECTION
-?) SHOW SUBFILE SIZE
 -The Subfile has  18918 Records.
-?find fn str orna
  -UNRECOGNIZED:  FN STR ORNA
-?find f str orna
  -RESULT: 22 SPECIMEN(S)
-?type

   MUSEUM-NUMBER = G103.54;
   CATALOGUE = FOSSIL;
   LOCALITY = UNKNOWN;
   GEOL-HORIZON = CAMPS SHALES;
   PERIOD = UNKNOWN;
   GEN-GRID-REF = 785.106;
   COLLECTOR-NAME = STAN WOOD;
   MISCELLANEOUS = TEMP. EXPOSURE;
   MISCELLANEOUS = REF ZOO REF W78;
   FOSSIL-DETAILS;
   FOSSIL-NAME = RHADINICHTHYS ORNATISSIMUS;
      PHYLUM = CHORDATA;
      OTHER-TAXA = PISCES;

   MUSEUM-NUMBER = G103.53;
   CATALOGUE = FOSSIL;
   LOCALITY = CRAIGLEIGH QUARRY EDINBURGH;
   GEOL-HORIZON = ABBEYHILL SHALES (VISEAN);
   PERIOD = UNKNOWN;
   COLLECTOR-NAME = STAN WOOD;
   MISCELLANEOUS = REF ZOO REF W59;
   FOSSIL-DETAILS;
   FOSSIL-NAME = RHADINICHTHYS ORNATISSIMUS;
      PHYLUM = CHORDATA;
      OTHER-TAXA = PISCES;
```

Reproduced with the permission of the Hancock Museum

Other ways of utilizing the information resources of the museum more effectively which are envisaged include producing listings of particular groups of specimens for interchange of information with experts elsewhere, and the publication of specialized booklets.

● *The British Museum (Natural History) London*

The Natural History Museum exemplifies the distinctive character of national museums as compared with regional ones. While regional museums' natural history departments are moving increasingly towards becoming centres for ecological site information, the national museums' collections remain essentially taxonomic. This is consistent with their role as the major repositories and with the research use which is made of them.

Almost all the search requests which the museum has to handle are on the lines 'What holdings have you of a given group of organisms' — ie item questions. The basic search strategy is thus from name to accession number to location in the museum. The major files of data are ordered by name, and the most common supplement required is a file ordered by country.

The simplicity of the search requirements has influenced the museum's approach to computer use. While the size of the collections makes computer handling of data appropriate, it was found, from early experimental work with the GOS-predecessor programs (the CGDS programs developed at the Sedgwick Museum) that they posed more complex input problems than appeared at first sight.

An analysis was therefore made of the ways in which it was needed to access the collections for the kind of use foreseen for the future. This led to decisions on a structure which would allow the meeting of the defined needs in the simplest possible way. Initially the CGDS package was used to meet these needs, but it was replaced over a period of three years by a set of specially prepared programs. Output from the programs is in the form of catalogues and indexes, by name, and occasionally by some other entry.

Some use is also made of microforms: for instance details of the ocean sediment collections, mainly from the Challenger expedition, have been published in microfiche, bound in book format, to enable research workers and other museums to decide what is of interest to them. Similarly 'swop lists' of pollen slides, which are prepared in duplicate, are put on fiche as a quick aid to other museums.

● References

Couprie, L D 'Iconclass, a device for the iconographical analysis of art objects' *Museum* XXX (3/4) 1978, 194—8

Cutbill, J L *Computer filing systems for museums and research* IRGMA, 1973

Institute of Agricultural History and Museum of English Rural Life *Museum procedures: trade records collection* by Phillips, D C University of Reading, 1973

Institute of Agricultural History and Museum of English Rural Life *Museum procedures: photographs* by Ward, S B, University of Reading, 1978

Institute of Agricultural History and Museum of English Rural Life *Museum procedure: classification,* University of Reading, 1978

Kirk, J J 'Using a computer in Brighton's museums' *Museums journal* 79 (1) June 1979, 17–20

MacKie, E W a) 'A hierarchy of artifact names for the MDA cards' *MDA information* 2(6) September 1978, 55–59
b) 'A hierarchy of artifact names for the MDA cards' (part 2) *MDA information* 2(7) October 1978, 66–70

North of England Open Air Museum *Classification of museum collections,* Second edition Beamish, 1980

Porter, M F, Light, R B & Roberts, D A *A unified approach to the computerization of museum catalogues* Report No. 5338 HC British Library, 1977

Price, D *The Sedgwick museum* Sedgwick Museum, 1979

Smither, R *Archive Preservation Programme And Retrieval by Automated Techniques* Department of Information Retrieval, Imperial War Museum, 1975

Smither, R 'Using APPARAT: Cataloguing film and sound recordings at the Imperial War Museum' *Aslib proceedings* 31 (4) April 1979, 170–79

Stone, S M 'St Albans museum documentation project' *Museums journal* 78(3) December 1978, 117–19

Stone, S M 'MDA user experience – St Albans Museum' *MDA information* 3(7) November 1979, 49–54

Bibliography

A selective list of books and articles which supplements the references quoted in the text.

● Background to IRGMA/MDA

Lewis, G D 'Information retrieval for museums'
Museums journal 67(2) September 1967, 88—91

Lewis, G D 'Information retrieval for museums'
Museums journal 69(3) December 1969, 142

Lewis, G D 'Information retrieval for museums'
Museums journal 70(3) December 1970, 134

Lewis, G D 'The information retrieval group of the Museums Association' *Museums journal* 71(3) December 1971, 129

Lewis, G D 'IRGMA' *Museums journal* 72(3) December 1972, 116

Lewis, G D 'IRGMA' *Museums journal* 73(3) December 1973, 128

Lewis, G D 'IRGMA' *Museums journal* 75(3) December 1975, 124

'Ten years of IRGMA 1967—1977' *Museums journal* 77(1)
June 1977, 11—14

Smurthwaite, D K *Museum information survey: a report examining the feasibility of a Museum Documentation Centre for the UK* Leicester, Leicester University, Department of Museum Studies, 1971

Museum Documentation Association *MDA news* (3/year) June 1977—

Museum Documentation Association *MDA information (monthly)* April 1977—

- Principles of library classification

Buchanan, B *Theory of library classification* Bingley, 1979

- Museum classifications

Blackwood, B *The classification of artefacts in the Pitt Rivers Museum Oxford* Pitt Rivers Museum Occasional Papers on Technology, II Oxford, Oxford University Press, 1970

Royal Anthropological Institute *Suggestions concerning the classification, storage and labelling of objects illustrating English life and traditions* Royal Anthropological Institute, 1950

- Museum documentation

Choudhury, A R *Art museum documentation and practical handling* Hyderabad, Choudhury & Choudhury, 1963

Oddon, Y *Elements of museum documentation* Jos (Nigeria), Jos Museum, 1968

Zaheer, M *Museum management. Accession, indexing, custody, labelling and verification of objects* Lucknow, Ram Advani, 1963

- Systems analysis and design

Mumford, E and Henshall, D *A participative approach to computer systems design* Associated Business Publications, 1978

Townley, H M *Systems analysis for information retrieval* Institute of Information Scientists Monograph Series, André Deutsch, 1978

- Optical coincidence cards

Gribble, M G 'The economics of information retrieval at Buxton Museum' *Museums journal* 72(1) June 1972, 21–2

● Computer use*

Bergengren, G 'Automatic data processing in the registration of museum objects in Sweden' *Museum* 23(1) 1970/71, 53–8

Chenhall, R G 'Museums and computers: a progress report' *Museum* XXX (1) 1978, 52–4

Cutbill, J L 'Computers as aids to museum documentation' *Museums journal* 74(3) December 1974, 115–16

Gittins, D 'Computer-based museum information systems' *Museums journal* 76(3) December 1976, 115–18

Museum XXX(3/4) 1978; issue devoted to 'Museums and computers'

Porter, Martin F 'Aspects of GOS' *MDA information* 2(3) June 1978, 21–6

Roberts, D A 'MDA computing facilities' *MDA information* 3(5) September 1979, 35

Whitehead, J B 'Developments in word processing systems and their application to information needs' *Aslib proceedings* 32 (3) March 1980, 118–133

● Archaeological site records

Hirst, S *Recording on excavations I: the written record* Hertford, Rescue, 1976

Jefferies, J S *Excavation records: techniques in use by the Central Excavation Unit* Directorate of Ancient Monuments and Historic Records, Occasional Papers No.1, Department of the Environment, 1977

● Biological records

Flood, S 'Museums as biological record centres' *Museums journal* 75(1) June 1975, 27–8

---

* The Computer Group of Aslib (Association of Special Libraries and Information Bureaux) organizes courses and seminars on the use of computers in information handling. Details from Aslib, 3 Belgrave Square, London SW1X 8PL

Suppliers of information retrieval packages referred to

● MINISIS
Information Sciences Division
International Development Research Centre
60 Great Queen Street
PO Box 8500
Ottawa
Canada K1G 3H9

● STATUS
ICL Dataskil Ltd
Reading Bridge House
Reading Bridge Approach
Reading RG1 8PN

● CAIRS
Leatherhead Food Research Association
Randalls Road
Leatherhead
Surrey KT22 7RY

● FACTFINDER
MCS Mini-computer Systems Ltd
Park House
Park Street
Maidenhead
Berkshire

● ASSASSIN
Management Services Department
Imperial Chemical Industries Ltd
PO Box 1
Billingham
Cleveland TS23 1LB

Index

abbreviations 107
access to information 7
  — access requirements 31-5, 46-54
  — contribution of indexes 17, 20
  — problems of access 30-31
  — through subject 46
alternative terms 60
APPARAT package 175
archaeological sites 150-52
archaeology collections 160-64
archives 175-6
art collections 143-4, 146

batch operation 93
BCPL 95
Beamish North of England Open Air
  Museum 155, 157-9
Birmingham City Museum 154-5, 156
Brighton museums 173-4
British Museum, Ethnography
  Department 167-8
British Museum (Natural History) 179

case studies 143-80
catalogues 11-12, 21
  — classified 22, 46, 77
  — computer-produced 99, 102, 114,
    121, 161, 169-70, 172, 174, 175, 177
  — information problems 30
  — lists 11
  — multiple 11-12, 46
cataloguing
  — books 9-10
  — museum objects 2, 9-10, 108-109
classification 12-21, 46, 56
  — Decimal Classification 13
  — 'distributed relative' 16-17, 30
  — faceted 15-16, 20, 22, 32
  — family tree 14
  — hierarchic 13-15, 16
  — indexes as complement to
    classification 16-20, 22, 47-8
  — libraries 12-20
  — museums 12-13, 20, 46, 144-5
    147, 155, 157, 165-7

  — notation 13, 21
  — principles of grouping 13
  — purposes 13
  — traditional 13-15, 16
COBOL 174
codes 107-108
COMfiche 121, 164, 174, 175-6
communication 130-33
computer-based information systems
  — abbreviations 107
  — catalogues 99, 102, 114, 121, 161,
    169-70, 172, 174, 175, 177, 179
  — cataloguers 97
  — choice of installation 92-4
  — codes 107-108
  — confidentiality 118
  — curators 97
  — data banks 113-14
  — data capture 103-109
  — data input documents 104-108
  — data preparation 109-11
  — data processing 112-19
  — data standards 103-104
  — elements 88-9
  — 'grandfather-father-son' tapes
    115-16
  — hardware 91-4
  — indexes 52, 54, 114, 161-4, 172
    174, 175, 177, 178, 179
  — information searches 118-19, 122
  — input 111-12
  — interactive systems 93-4
  — management 88-128
  — microforms 121
  — monitoring 122-4
  — objectives 89-90
  — on-line access to data banks 118-19
  — operating modes 93-4
  — output 119-20
  — printers 119-20
  — publication of data 118
  — security 115-18
  — software 89, 94-6, 152-3, 160-73
  — staff involvement 4, 89, 90, 96-8
  — standards manuals 108-109

185